Legal Self-Defense for
Mental Health Practitioners

Robert Henley Woody, PhD, ScD, JD, received the Doctor of Philosophy degree from Michigan State University, the Doctor of Science degree from the University of Pittsburgh, and the Juris Doctor degree from Creighton University. He completed postdoctoral studies at the University of London and the Washington School of Psychiatry. He is a member of the Florida, Michigan, and Nebraska Bars, and is a Licensed Psychologist in Florida and Michigan. He is a Fellow of the American Psychological Association, and a Diplomate in Clinical and Forensic Psychology (ABPP) and a Diplomate in Psychological Assessment (ABAP).

After professorial stints at the State University of New York at Buffalo, the University of Maryland, the Ohio University, and the Grand Valley State University, in 1975 Dr. Woody became a Professor of Psychology at the University of Nebraska at Omaha (he is a former Dean for Graduate Studies and Research there). He has consistently maintained independent private practices in both law and psychology. Over his three decades-plus as an attorney, he has advised, counseled, represented, and taught courses and seminars to mental health practitioners from all of the professional disciplines.

Dr. Woody graduated from the Pat Thomas Law Enforcement Center (Tallahassee) and was a sworn law enforcement officer with the Florida Department of Law Enforcement. The National Rifle Association has named him a Certified Instructor of Pistol and Personal Protection in the Home.

Dr. Woody has previously authored/edited 34 books and over 200 articles and chapters.

Legal Self-Defense for Mental Health Practitioners

Quality Care and Risk Management Strategies

Robert Henley Woody, PhD, ScD, JD

SPRINGER PUBLISHING COMPANY
NEW YORK

Springer Publishing Company, LLC
11 West 42nd Street
New York, NY 10036
www.springerpub.com

Acquisitions Editor: Nancy Hale
Production Editor: Joseph Stubenrauch
Composition: diacriTech

ISBN: 978-0-8261-9565-4
e-book ISBN: 978-0-8261-9566-1

12 13 14 15 / 5 4 3 2 1

The author and the publisher of this Work have made every effort to use sources believed to be reliable to provide information that is accurate and compatible with the standards generally accepted at the time of publication. The author and publisher shall not be liable for any special, consequential, or exemplary damages resulting, in whole or in part, from the readers' use of, or reliance on, the information contained in this book. The publisher has no responsibility for the persistence or accuracy of URLs for external or third-party Internet websites referred to in this publication and does not guarantee that any content on such websites is, or will remain, accurate or appropriate.

Library of Congress Cataloging-in-Publication Data

Woody, Robert Henley.

  Legal self-defense for mental health practitioners : quality care and risk management strategies / Robert Henley Woody.

    p. cm.

  Includes bibliographical references and index.

  ISBN 978-0-8261-9565-4 (alk. paper)

  1. Mental health personnel--Malpractice. 2. Mental health personnel--Professional ethics. I. Title.

  RC440.8.W6594 2012

  616.890068--dc23

                    2012013910

Printed in the United States of America by Gasch Printing.

To the mental health practitioners with whom, as their attorney or consulting psychologist, I have shared the mission of quality care and risk management, and especially those who have suffered from nefariously motivated ethical and legal complaints and legal challenges.

Contents

Preface

For more than three decades, I have been an attorney providing legal counsel to mental health practitioners; that is, psychologists, mental health counselors, clinical social workers, marriage and family therapists, psychiatrists, and other ancillary professionals, such as psychiatric nurses, sex therapists, and various types of educators. Consequently, I have helped them improve practice strategies for achieving quality care, confronting ethics and licensing complaints, and defending against possible or actual legal challenges. I have found that mental health practitioners have unique characteristics and face problems that are not common to other types of health care professionals. Prior to becoming an attorney, I had been a psychologist and health care professional, which adds to my perspective. Throughout my career, I have been a professor, which led to my conducting seminars and teaching undergraduate and graduate courses on ethics and law.

In this book, I share my knowledge and experiences about maintaining quality care and protecting the personal and legal rights of service recipients (also known as service users, clients, consumers, and patients—these terms will be used interchangeably in this book) and mental health practitioners. I will uncover the legal risks of being a mental health practitioner in this day and age.

Given "political correctness," this book is different from many other books about the legal aspects of mental health services, because it does not hold the rights of the recipient of mental health services to be singularly supreme.

Rather, it recognizes that the professional relationship involving a mental health practitioner and a client or patient should honor the rights of BOTH parties.

The central thesis is that modern mental health practitioners must be cognizant of negative responses from a client or patient. Such responses from a service user may include: failure to abide by policies (including for payments) agreed on at the outset of professional services, not adhering to an individualized treatment plan that embraces essential professional requirements for quality care and risk management, demonstrating inappropriate aggression (i.e., hostile and violent actions), and threatening or filing unjustified ethics and licensing complaints and/or lawsuits.

By definition, every profession should go through substantial changes in order to accommodate shifts in public policies, laws, and the needs of society. As the mental health professions have evolved, the definition, scope of service, required qualifications, ethics, standards, and laws have changed dramatically. This book emphasizes two aspects of the contemporary framework for the mental health practitioner, regardless of discipline: (1) providing safeguards from problems and (2) protecting the rights of BOTH the mental health practitioner and the service user.

Before becoming an attorney, I was a mental health practitioner. Beyond my basic mental health doctoral program (PhD, Michigan State University), postdoctoral training in clinical psychology (University of London) and group psychotherapy (Washington School of Psychiatry), and another doctoral program in public health (ScD, University of Pittsburgh), my ideas about mental health services changed substantially after I completed a law degree (JD, Creighton University). Contrary to the original definition of "professionalism," practitioners are no longer the primary source for regulation of a service discipline. Like it or not, current health-related professionalism is subject to legal monitoring and control by government agencies, third-party payment sources, and the court system.

I have been blessed by a solid law practice, pretty much limited to advising, counseling, representing, and teaching mental health practitioners from all of the disciplines who face dissatisfied and accusatory service users, allegations of ethical and licensure infractions, and threats of legal challenges (e.g., malpractice actions). Providing legal services to practitioners increased my appreciation of the benefits that mental health professionals bring to society. I also have come to recognize, however, that society has adopted some faulty beliefs about mental health services.

My practice of the law has revealed that courts of law generally protect the rights of equal protection and due process, as guaranteed by the United States Constitution. Through astute legislation and under the watchful eye of the judiciary, the mental health practitioner facing a lawsuit is likely to get a just and fair "day in court."

With ethics and licensing complaints, especially licensing boards within state government (given the powerful political motive), equal protection and due process for mental health practitioners are not as assured. The conditions in government monitoring and discipline often are similar in the deliberations of ethics committees within a professional association. Because the relationship between a practitioner and a service user has been joined by government and third-party payment sources, the monitoring of quality care too often shows deference to consumers (some of whom are quite pathological), resulting in what amounts to abuse of or at least jeopardy for the practitioner's personal and legal rights.

At the federal and state levels, regulatory law governs professional practices. Through legislation (e.g., statutes and administrative code rules), governmental agencies define the qualifications for practitioners, the services and practices that can be offered, the system for monitoring the mandatory quality of care, and impose discipline on offending practitioners (e.g., restricting or removing the privilege of practicing provided by licensure). For disreputable reasons, some complainants misuse the regulatory law system—file false and malicious complaints—and in turn, the system allows the abuse of the system to happen. When brought into the regulatory law system by a complaint to a licensing board, more than a few mental health practitioners have been unfairly treated legally and the discipline imposed failed to balance the legal rights of BOTH parties. Said bluntly, the Constitutional rights to be innocent until proven guilty, equal protection, and due process may be, for unjust and wrongful reasons, denied to the practitioner.

Mental health practitioners also must contend with professional ethics committees. I have had the honor of serving on several ethics committees for national- and state-level professional associations, and participating as a source of legal information for multiple committees that were drafting ethics codes. Regrettably, I have observed some members of ethics committees (and licensing boards as well) who are more motivated by personal ambition than by service to the public or the profession. Notions of self-importance and a "political correctness" mentality can contribute to a lack of objectivity (e.g., "If I can find fault with a colleague, it will prove my professional superiority to others").

Many mental health practitioners lack the wherewithal to protect themselves. Their training may not have prepared them to understand the legal and business aspects of practice in contemporary society. Training in all of the mental health professions typically emphasizes the welfare of the service user, but it is rare for there to be a focus on modern complex therapeutic relationship issues that may threaten the rights of the practitioner. It is an understatement to assert that mental health practitioners lack a much needed "warrior" mentality when facing allegations of wrongdoing or suffering improper conduct by a service user. A practitioner today needs to be prepared to stand firm and to assertively defend his or her rights, but a mindset of this nature and the relevant skills needed are seldom addressed or cultivated in professional training programs.

This book presents numerous actual cases (of course, name, gender, locale, etc., have been changed to protect anonymity) in which mental health practitioners needed to be mindful of protecting themselves and to implement safeguards proactively. Incidentally, having worked in numerous state jurisdictions and being familiar with published legal cases, the cases mentioned were selected to present a national scope. The information in this book brings ideas about mental health principles, ethics, standards, and laws out of the Ivory Tower and into the sunlight of reality.

ONE

Mental Health Practitioners Under Siege

Modern societies have unrelenting commitment to promoting constructive, healthy, and rewarding conditions for all people—there is a quest for excellence of life. Regrettably, there is reason to believe that there may be unrealistic expectations that, when unfulfilled, lead to frustration that could accommodate faulty reasoning (Stewart, 2010). For example, the high incidence of mental disorders, as broadly defined, in the United States may be a concomitant of stress and frustration (World Health Organization World Mental Health Survey Consortium, 2004). Logically, when there is a problem, the society focuses on finding remedies, such as relying on government to implement solutions.

Health-related problems have led to marked changes in professionalism relevant to mental health services. By definition, a "profession" is required to benefit society. Based on public policy and law, the government and members of a profession are united in an ongoing effort to ensure that everyone who is granted the privilege to be deemed a professional has the potential to bring benefits to society.

Mental health practitioners must cultivate competency to provide effective services. Through training, ethics, and laws, there are expectations that the practitioner will ensure quality care and maximize the possibility of being helpful to consumers.

In the last half century, society has become increasingly accepting of and dependent on the mental health professions. Social status and financial rewards are accorded to those who complete extensive training, prove to be of acceptable character, and give evidence of knowledge and skills that will be transformed into helpful professional services.

In the last half century, society has become increasingly accepting of and dependent on the mental health professions. Social status and financial rewards are accorded to those who complete extensive training, prove to be of acceptable character, and give evidence of knowledge and skills that will be transformed into helpful professional services.

As with any component of society, it is necessary to scrutinize what is and is not occurring, with the objective being to remedy any problem and create additional safeguards for all concerned. However, there is a major dilemma within the mental health professions, which has not been attended to adequately by either society or the professions. This dilemma allows noncompliant clients to jeopardize quality care and impose unjustified risks on mental health practitioners. (The terms service users, patients, consumers, and clients will be used interchangeably in this book.)

Until the mid-1970s, society generally held mental health professionals in high regard. Due to some unfortunate situations and questionable practices by some professionals, considerable suspicion developed toward the integrity of those in the health care industry. There will be further discussion of this assertion later on, among several chapters, including Chapter Three.

Incidentally, some professional associations and malpractice carriers now provide "hot-lines" for legal consultation. One of the risks of contacting a "hot-line" attorney provided by a professional association or malpractice carrier is that the information or advice provided may emphasize professional ethics that are not necessarily compatible with the laws of the jurisdiction(s) relevant to the particular mental health practitioner. State bar associations typically advise consumers to seek legal counsel from an attorney qualified in the given jurisdiction. Also, a "hot-line" attorney may be paid by a malpractice carrier that is, by definition, a financial institution intent on preserving the fiscal assets of the organizations, as opposed to primarily protecting the legal interests of the insured who is calling for advice. This caveat will be repeated purposefully later on.

Therefore, modern mental health practitioners must be cognizant of negative responses from clients. For example, clients may: fail to abide by or comply with policies agreed on at the outset of professional services (e.g., making timely payments); not adhere to an individualized treatment plan that embraces essential professional requirements for quality care and risk management; be inappropriately aggressive (e.g., making threats, acting hostile, or becoming violent); and file unjustified ethics and licensing complaints and/or lawsuits. Consider the following three examples:

EXAMPLE ONE

When pressed to pay an overdue account, a former service user said: "Either you forget the debt or I am going to inform the licensing board that you billed for sessions that did not occur." The practitioner said, "But I have notes for those sessions and they did occur." The abusive service user replied, "I will say that you falsified those notes, and you know who the licensing board will believe—certainly not you."

EXAMPLE TWO

An highly disturbed service user, who, from the practitioner's records, was clearly a risk to self and others, rejected the mental health practitioner's good faith attempt to terminate outpatient sessions and obtain an inpatient placement. The service user declared, "If you try to get me committed involuntarily or refuse to keep seeing me on an outpatient basis, I will have a malpractice lawyer all over your ass."

EXAMPLE THREE

A senior practitioner terminated an employee-practitioner for indisputable dishonesty and breach of the terms and conditions in the legally well-crafted employment contract. In retaliation, the terminated practitioner filed both ethics and licensing complaints against the employer, with a number of false allegations. Interestingly, the licensing board dismissed the complaint, but the professional ethics committee pursued the complaint and based its penalizing decision on an ethical tenet that was contradicted by the laws of the relevant jurisdiction.

Throughout the health care professions, there has been a proliferation of malpractice lawsuits by disgruntled patients (Shapiro & Smith, 2011). Some of these legal actions were well justified, whereas some were for less than honorable reasons (e.g., a highly disturbed client attempting to gain unjust enrichment or pursuing pathological motivations via accusations against the mental health practitioner).

From a legal perspective, there seems to be adequate reason to believe that, in general, any lawsuit that reaches the courtroom will, in fact, receive justice. When there is a seemingly illogical outcome in a court of law, it most often results from a "jury of one's peers" disbelieving or being shocked by the evidence presented and occasionally as a result of inept lawyering.

Overall, legislatures have crafted wise laws that the judiciary administers well in courtroom proceedings. The outcome usually has ensured equal protection and due process, and justice is done. For mental health practitioners, the same positive critique cannot be given to professional ethics committees or the regulatory law system (e.g., the process of complaints to a licensing board).

In most states, a mental health regulatory agency, for example, the Department of Health, is almost exclusively a source of consumer advocacy and protection. This agency contains the licensing board(s) for the practice of mental health services.

Mental health practitioners delude themselves into believing that, because licensing enhances their professional status (which may or may not be true) and there are mental health professionals on the licensing board(s), the regulatory agency is a source of professional advocacy and protection for the practitioner. Nothing could be further from the truth.

The members of a state licensing board commonly are appointed by the governor, which makes it a political position. Talking to board members quickly reveals that they believe that their role is to police the marketplace, often with a "guilty until proven innocent" attitude.

Complaints made to the licensing board usually are investigated. In some jurisdictions, the investigators often are trained as law enforcement officers and have little or no training in mental health services per se. If the complaint appears plausible for discipline following the investigation, it is then assigned to a prosecuting attorney. Within the prosecutorial framework, any service user can contact the regulatory agency, file a complaint (sometimes without being under oath and/or by an "800" toll-free number), and have an investigation initiated.

Any number of times in my experience, the person making the complaint (the complainant) has admitted later to falsehoods or misrepresentations in the allegations, but virtually never does the regulatory agency take action against the consumer—it would not be politically correct. Out of several hundred licensing complaints for which I have provided legal representation, there has never been, to my knowledge, any effort by a licensing board or prosecutor to hold a complainant responsible for falsehoods. In the meantime, the mental health practitioner who has been the subject of the wrongful licensing complaint has suffered emotionally and financially; often the practitioner's professional reputation is tarnished, even though the allegations were discredited. For example, one respondent who sued the licensing board and won told me that the aftermath resulted in a marked decline in referrals and income in every subsequent year. I have heard similar stories from numerous practitioners.

Commonly the complainant in a licensing complaint enjoys some sort of statutory protection from a counteraction by the practitioner. That is, unless it can be proven clearly by at least a preponderance of the evidence that the complainant has filed a complaint that was knowingly false and malicious, the mental health practitioner must face the taxpayer supported investigation and prosecution without pragmatic recourse. Certain regulatory sources, such as licensing board members and even prosecuting attorneys, have commiserated about this problem, but quickly say, "If the practitioner wants to sue the complainant, fine, but don't expect us to be involved against the complainant." Again, it would not be politically savvy for a consumer protection agency to defend the practitioner and oppose the consumer.

Note that the attorney representing the regulatory agency is, in fact, termed a "prosecuting attorney." One prosecutor told me that she was amazed at the naiveté of mental health practitioners who have received a licensing complaint. She said, "So many of them call and confess their sins to me, as if I would grant them forgiveness—I now start every letter or telephone conversation with the statement 'I am a prosecutor and you should obtain your own legal counsel because anything that you tell me can and will be used against you.'"

A complaint without merit can lead to additional problems. Prosecutors have been known to use a complaint about one issue to expand the investigation in fishing-expedition style to other issues, which they might detect from reviewing clinical records.

Moreover, one state statute grants immunity from a licensing complaint to court-appointed child custody evaluators and parenting coordinators, unless a disgruntled parent first takes the matter to the appointing judge and the judge declares the evaluator to have performed unsatisfactorily. However, the prosecutorial unit in that state acknowledges that, should a parent file a complaint against a court-appointed child custody evaluator or parent coordinator without getting the judicial finding of unsatisfactory performance, the parent will be asked, in effect, "Is there anything else that you can complain about that alleges a lack of good faith on the part of the evaluator or coordinator!" The reasoning is clear: The complaint process is for consumer protection. Remember, prosecutors and the like receive salary increases, promotions, and job security according to "successful" prosecutions and consumer satisfaction.

Many practitioners report that a regulatory action is more devastating to them than a malpractice suit. This is because courtroom proceedings must adhere strictly to formal rules (e.g., the Rules of Evidence, Civil Procedure, or Criminal Procedure), legal representation by an attorney is ensured by the U.S. Constitution, and appeals can be made.

DAMAGES FROM COMPLAINTS

Research shows that mental health practitioners who are subjected to any ethics, regulatory, or legal action suffer mightily, with the effects being mental and physical symptoms, marital and family distress, and financial loss (Woody, 2009b). Nothing cuts to the core of a practitioner's identity more than an assault on his or her professionalism. When the practitioner knows that the complaint is false and comes from a client's pathology, and there is dubious legal recourse (with the stance of "guilty until proven innocent"), the negative impact on the practitioner is all too often horrendous.

Research shows that mental health practitioners who are subjected to any ethics, regulatory, or legal action suffer mightily, with the effects being mental and physical symptoms, marital and family distress, and financial loss (Woody, 2009b).

One practitioner said: "I was burned royally by my licensing board—completely vindicated, even received a monetary award from the psychology board by an administrative law judge for the egregious prosecution. But I still suffer from the years of lost productivity and hundreds of thousands of dollars in lost income while fighting the case." Welch (2010) believes that "psychologists are one angry patient, parent or spouse away from professional ruin" (p. 15).

The mental health practitioner today is without adequate allies. It is erroneous to believe that a professional association will be assuredly understanding of the dilemma that the practitioner faces in the legal arena and step forward to offer support. For example, it would not be expedient politically to champion the cause of a member accused of wrongdoing, because it might impact negatively on legislative priorities being pursued by the professional association. Of course, an adverse judgment from an ethics committee, a licensing board, or a malpractice court could tarnish the reputation of the profession in general. The old saw about "rats leaving a sinking ship" comes to mind.

I have seen numerous cases in which a regulatory agency dismissed a complaint for lack of probable cause or a court of law dismissed a malpractice action, yet a professional association continued investigating an ethics complaint, sometimes extending the investigation over several years. Some practitioners who have faced multiple tribunals report that they believe that a professional association, much like a licensing board, tends to see the practitioner as guilty until proven innocent.

Because of the negative attributions seen in ethics committees in professional associations, some practitioners have chosen to cease their memberships. In a nutshell, the ethics model for a decision about a violation is considerably different from the model used for licensing and malpractice actions; more will be said about these differences later on. Suffice it to say, ethics committees are prone to want pristine conduct. Idealism tends to dictate the decision, with little consideration of the realities of practice. Welch (2010) opined: "It is unfortunate that they [psychologists] have to fear . . . [professional ruin] from their national organization, but the sad truth is that they do" (p. 15).

> Although only a minimum risk at one time, ethics and licensing complaints and malpractice litigation against mental health practitioners now impose a profound risk. The published frequency of complaints and lawsuits is usually based on only the cases that actually are submitted to ethics committees, licensing boards, and malpractice insurance carriers. Even when these numbers are combined with the annual reports, such as from state regulatory agencies, the total does not reveal the true magnitude or incidence of legal problems faced by practitioners.

When it comes to malpractice, recipients of mental health services enjoy a wide doorway into the halls of justice. With the prevailing attitudes and prosecutorial governmental system, the hope that the matter will end "in justice" is overly optimistic.

Although only a minimum risk at one time, ethics and licensing complaints and malpractice litigation against mental health practitioners now impose a profound risk. The published frequency of complaints and lawsuits is usually based on only the cases that actually are submitted to ethics committees, licensing boards, and malpractice insurance carriers. Even when these numbers are combined with the annual reports, such as from state regulatory agencies, the total does not reveal the true magnitude or incidence of legal problems faced by practitioners.

It is important to emphasize that reliable information regarding the number of allegations and complaints of any type cannot be obtained. Many potential complaints or lawsuits are settled, usually financially, without ever being filed, thus eliminating them from the tabulations. My law clients have told me of countless situations in which a mental health service user (usually one from whom the practitioner is trying to collect a justified overdue debt) states unabashedly: "If a settlement of X-amount is not received, a complaint to the licensing board and/or a law suit will be filed." As I suggested earlier, some clients have even stated openly that they will fabricate alleged wrongdoing on the part of the practitioner, quickly adding, "Since it will be your word against mine, I'll have the system on my side." Again, it is impossible to tabulate the number of legal actions, because settlements involving mental health practitioners are not always reported to the state government or anywhere else.

When it comes to using the legal system, it seems that some service users are better versed and prepared for a legal skirmish than mental health practitioners. Steeped in the Ivory Tower illogic that a client always must be nurtured and shown deference, the mental health practitioner may be prone to experience inappropriate guilt. A practitioner might say to his or her attorney, "I know I did not do anything wrong, but I just want to get this over with, settle it however you can."

Stated bluntly, the present era allows service users with personality disorders and other serious pathology to abuse the legal and governmental systems to the disadvantage and injury of mental health practitioners. Moreover, the practitioner is left with too few allies and resources. This state of affairs should shock the sensibilities of every member of society, the mental health professions, and training programs and trigger a desire for corrective actions. The unjust psychological injury, diminished professional status, and financial penalties suffered by modern mental health practitioners are appalling.

RECONCEPTUALIZING MENTAL HEALTH SERVICES PRACTICE

There are strategies for avoiding ethical, regulatory, and legal problems, which I have detailed elsewhere (Woody, 1988a, 1988b, 1989, 1991, 2000b, 2005, 2008, to name but a few). These strategies require knowledge, skills, and attitudes that are seldom, if ever, dealt with adequately in professional training programs. It is known that training for ethics, standards, and law can reduce misconduct (Price, 2010). Nonetheless, there is a dearth of essential training experiences of this nature.

Part of the problem is that university and other types of professional training programs emphasize the ethics model and ignore or downplay the legal aspects of professional practice. This may be because, in part, some professors are not versed enough in the law or the reality of practice.

Certainly trainees should develop ethical, theoretical, and idealistic ideas, but they also should learn that mental health is now part of the Health Care Industry. In addition to government oversight (which seems destined to increase), mental health practices are subject to managed health care systems and other third-party payment sources. Consequently, business and clinical acumen should be of equal importance. The professional service relationship must be reconceptualized as involving not only the practitioner and the service user, but numerous other accountability sources, such as professional liability companies, health insurance companies, ethics committees, regulatory agencies, and malpractice courts: Training should be adapted and provided accordingly. Reconceptualizing mental health services practice also must include a commitment to continual enrichment of knowledge and refinement of skills by self study and continuing education that is reality oriented.

Affiliations between mental health practitioners must be based on business principles—contracts, corporate entities, policies—not simply on collegiality. While quality care must be maintained for the benefit of the consumer, it must also be maintained to protect the practitioner from the risk of complaints and lawsuits. Just as medical physicians already do, mental health practitioners, regardless of discipline or theoretical preferences, must use diagnostics in a clinical way to improve judgments, that is, avoid biases, and preclude ethical, regulatory, and legal complaints. Compliance with an individualized treatment plan should be required. If the consumer does not adhere strictly to policies

9

and treatment procedures, a therapeutic method should be used to deal with the noncompliance and, if all else fails, termination of the services. Justification for and the propriety of such actions should be documented in the records.

These ideas for reconceptualizing mental health services practices will be discussed further in later chapters. In no way should this reconceptualization be viewed as lessening the potential benefits to society or the individual service user. On the contrary, by giving equal concern to the quality of care to the service user and the legal rights and protection of the mental health practitioner, the mental health professions are strengthened and individuals and society benefit even more.

CONCLUSION

None of the foregoing is intended to be disrespectful or a wholesale condemnation of the mental health professions, university and other training programs, or the ethical, regulatory, and legal systems. Rather, the intention is to reveal that mental health services in the 21st century have changed, and that training and practice also must change to address the reality of societal and professional conditions.

I suggest that any antiquated notions about mental health services be discarded. The service user must demonstrate appropriate adherence to operational and treatment policies and plans; the mental health practitioner must offer well defined and evidence-based services (preferably with support from empirical research); and society must view professional mental health services as being similar to other business-related service relationships, except for clearly relevant ethical, regulatory, and legal prescriptions and proscriptions.

After enduring ethical and licensing complaints and legal challenges, too many mental health practitioners are prone to engage in "crying the blues," which accomplishes nothing more than catharsis. Instead, all mental health practitioners should lead the effort to reshape the regulatory and accountability sources, through political and legislative efforts, seeking at a minimum equal protection for the client and the practitioner alike.

In part because of the indoctrination that occurs in the name of professionalism during training programs, the typical mental health practitioner is not able to effectively combat criticism generally, and ethical and regulatory complaints and legal challenges specifically. When faced with opposition, many mental health practitioners find it almost impossible to stand their ground and assert their own rights, such as the right of privacy, equal protection, and due process. Clinging to outdated notions, these practitioners disregard proactively implementing legal strategies.

Over and over, practitioners involved with ethical, regulatory, or legal actions have said, "When this mess is wrapped up, you can bet that I am going to become active in changing the system." Almost without exception, when the complaint proceedings are over, the practitioner senses such relief that he or she does not want to even think about the situation any more (Sigmund Freud was right about the principle of repression), or expend his or her last remnants of energy on trying to change the system.

In this book, my intention is to enlist the reader in pledging to work toward adopting and maintaining legal strategies for: (1) maintenance of quality care; (2) risk management; and (3) balanced and equal protection for mental health practitioners and their clients. The objectives require open-mindedness and the creation of safeguards against actions by contemporary ethical, regulatory, and legal monitoring and accountability systems. Perhaps with a joining of forces, mental health practitioners from various disciplines can bring about needed systemic changes, such as improved procedures within professional associations and legislative directives and administrative rules. This kind of social action requires the ability and willingness to firmly protect ethical responsibilities and legal rights. Constructive "professional warriorism" is not a hostile-aggressive objective, it is a self-defense approach to professional practice, which will protect and benefit all concerned, including society.

> *Perhaps with a joining of forces, mental health practitioners from various disciplines can bring about needed systemic changes, such as improved procedures within professional associations and legislative directives and administrative rules.*

TWO

The Social Psychology of Practitioner Vulnerability: Avoiding Psychological Errors

When a service user begins to feel negatively toward a mental health practitioner, the cause of the dissatisfaction may be rooted in the service user's character disorder or pathology, or it may be due to something that the practitioner did or did not do. Poor quality professional services can occur by omission or commission. Consequently, there must be a consistent and studied approach by the mental health practitioner to avoid any weakness or flaw in the quality of the professional services.

The threshold issue for the practitioner is being sensitive to what is occurring and the effects that are produced. As Barlow (2010) says, "Most therapists would agree that it is crucial to be concerned about and sensitive to harmful effects, however small" (p. 18). Any negative effects may be due to unrelated life events, adverse therapeutic influence, or the way that the psychological treatment interacts with the client's idiosyncratic variables (Bergin & Strupp, 1972).

Logically, in mental health services, there are ever-present judgments being made, such as what communications to initiate with the client and how to respond to the client. The decision making by the practitioner is highly subjective. Some decisions and concomitant actions may help and some may harm (Dimidjian & Hollon, 2010).

Indeed, Castonguay, Boswell, Constantino, Goldfried, and Hill (2010) state bluntly:

> However painful it may be, it is important for those of us who are psychotherapists to recognize that we have all likely harmed one or more of our clients . . . we would venture a guess that all experienced psychotherapists have, at one point or another in their careers, failed to meet the most basic and ethically important principle guiding the profession: First, do no harm. (p. 34)

There must be a consistent and studied approach to avoid any weakness or flaw in the quality of professional services, especially those that could emanate from personal qualities or limits of competence. This challenge can benefit from "emphasis on a more idiographic approach in methods and data analysis and a close collaboration among practitioners and clinical scientists" (Barlow, 2010, p. 18; see also Barlow & Nock, 2009). The idiographic approach "involves the thorough intensive study of a single person or case in order to obtain an in-depth understanding of that person or case, as contrasted with a study of the universal aspects of groups of people or cases" (VandenBos, 2007, p. 465).

There must be a consistent and studied approach to avoid any weakness or flaw in the quality of professional services, especially those that could emanate from personal qualities or limits of competence.

This chapter identifies the sources of high-risk actions by the practitioner, relying on principles of psychology to construct the backdrop for the protective shield that will be presented in all of the subsequent chapters. Consideration will be given to the nature and definition of psychological errors, determination of a psychological error, influence from personal characteristics of the practitioner (e.g., values, beliefs, and biases, professional ethics), and clinical versus statistical judgments. The final message will be that, to minimize risks that can lead to psychological errors, professional services must be based on scholarly and research evidence. In other words, I hope to offer you the means to embrace the old adage "forewarned is forearmed."

THE NATURE AND DEFINITION OF PSYCHOLOGICAL ERRORS

Regrettably, some mental health practitioners do, in fact, make errors in judgments and conduct, which I refer to as psychological errors. A "psychological error" refers to analyses, assessments, judgments, decisions, and actions taken by a practitioner that result in an unacceptable quality of service for a patient. In the context of psychological errors, the term "psychological" is applicable to all of the mental health disciplines.

The bed rock for determining a practice error is, in part, what a substantial portion of like professionals believe is appropriate or correct. This criterion is quite commonly present in tort cases (a "tort" case is a civil, not criminal, action alleging injury to person, property, or rights of the person), as well as in statutes and administrative code rules for the various mental health disciplines, depending on the legal idiosyncrasies of the particular jurisdiction(s) that are applicable to the practitioner. For example, Florida licensed psychologists can be disciplined for "Failing to meet the minimum standards of performance in professional activities when measured against generally prevailing peer performance, including the undertaking of activities for which the licensee is not qualified by training or experience" (Florida Statute 490.009(a)(r)).

A psychological error is likely to occur when the mental health practitioner deviates from true or accurate information, and can occur during assessment, intervention, or any other mental health service. Although the psychological error is most often due to faulty reasoning or judgment on the part of the practitioner, certain mental health methods have the potential for inherent errors, for example, psychological assessments. Van Ornum, Dunlap, and Shore (2008) issue the reminder that an error may be due to a statistical anomaly, misinformation, bias, or faulty judgment. The result will be an unsound decision that may not be appropriate or helpful to the service user. Error is "present within all assessments and refers to factors other than what the tool is designed to measure that may contribute to scores on a test" (p. 497). Of course mental health assessments include methods that are not "tests"

> A psychological error is likely to occur when the mental health practitioner deviates from true or accurate information, and can occur during assessment, intervention, or any other mental health service.

per se, such as "mental status" exams, and projective methods, which are also prone to error.

There are a myriad of possible psychological errors, including: improper diagnosis, failure to comply with mandatory abuse reporting laws, inadequate assessment of potential for violence (e.g., suicide, homicide), and failure to detect medical conditions presenting as a psychological or psychiatric disorder. A fertile area for error is treatment planning, that is, the practitioner fails to create a meaningful and appropriate treatment plan that will likely benefit the service user.

I believe that to minimize psychological errors the mental health practitioner should operate by five basic guidelines. First, there should be an effort to gain scholarly information about the historical and behavioral science bases for and critical terms pertaining to psychological errors. Second, there should be knowledge of principles for professional services based on (among other areas) social psychology. (Note: I have found research on social psychology to be extremely helpful for preparing mental health practitioners to identify and control potential sources of bias.) Third, the practitioner should accept the importance of maintaining objectivity. Fourth, the practitioner should understand how evidence-based professional services help prevent errors. Fifth, the practitioner should cultivate insights about how to identify, minimize, correct, and prevent psychological errors. These five guidelines underlie the substance of this chapter.

DETERMINATION OF A PSYCHOLOGICAL ERROR

In order for a psychological error to "occur," some authoritative source must make a judgment about an omission or commission on the part of a mental health practitioner. A declaration of an "error" presumably has a legal or ethical professional basis, such as a statute or administrative code rule pertaining to the practice of psychology, mental health counseling, marriage and family therapy, or clinical social work, or a standard within an ethics code from a professional association.

The basis for declaring a psychological error should be authoritative, detailed in an objective manner, and communicated to all relevant mental health practitioners prior to any authoritative source's making an allegation or judgment that the practitioner committed a psychological error. Fisher (2009) indicates that "adjudicatory decisions based on an ethics code remain vulnerable to overturn on appeal if defendants can argue that they had no forewarning that specific behaviors were ethical violations" (p. 21).

For licensed mental health practitioners, it is not uncommon to have allegations made by a service user to a state licensing board reflect idiosyncratic notions held (sometimes even conjured up) by a service user. In turn, the regulatory process, devoted to "consumer protection," may allow for the service user's reconstructive memory. The latter refers to the "perspective that memory is continually vulnerable to revision" (Bartol & Bartol, 2012, p. 387). Consumer protection sources often apply 20/20 hindsight when judging that conduct by the licensed mental health practitioner should be viewed as an error potentially deserving of disciplinary sanctions.

Even if a licensed mental health practitioner believes that a particular service is error free, opinions from other sources can impose condemnation, which can result in a career-long blemish on the practitioner's record of professionalism. This vulnerability underscores the importance of every licensed mental health practitioner implementing and maintaining legal safeguards, by adhering strictly to all statutes and administrative code rules, as well as professional standards and ethics, and exercising risk management to minimize the possibility of negativity and complaints.

VALUES, BELIEFS, AND BIASES

Values are held by individuals and collectives, and are: "Enduring beliefs about important life goals that transcend specific situations" (Franzoi, 2009, p. G-7). By definition, an "error" means that an authoritative source has determined that a value has been breached. For example, when a member of a licensing board (serving on a probable cause panel for determining a violation) decides, without the benefit of a well-defined law or standard, that an allegedly errant licensed mental health practitioner has committed a violation, the decision is connected to personally held values.

Personal values are general beliefs that certain ideas or behaviors are or are not acceptable, and these personal convictions influence mental health services:

> Psychological advice also reflects the advice giver's personal values. When mental health professionals advise us how to live

our lives, when child-rearing experts tell us how to handle our children, and when some psychologists encourage us to live free of concern for others' expectations, they are expressing their personal values. (Myers, 2005, p. 15)

According to Fiske (2004), values seem to derive from biological needs, interpersonal coordination, and group welfare. Putting value into the pro-social (benefits to others) context of psychology practice, it would mean:

Prosocial behavior can result from varying levels of moral rea-soning, which range from controlling outcomes and promot-ing self-interest to more collective concerns to understanding abstract moral principles. Specific personal norms can operate in a given situation, and more general moral values transcend situations. (p. 358)

In other words, the highly personal nature of values can impact on men-tal health practice, notwithstanding the practitioner's education, training, and commitment to ethics and law. Likewise, the values can determine and shape the beliefs about what is true and accepted by others that the mental health practitioner uses for personal and professional attributions.

Given the unique nature of mental health services, the term "attri-bution" merits clarification. Becoming a mental health practitioner neces-sitates deciding on personal values that are linked to professionalism. Franzoi (2009) defines attribution as: "The process by which people use information to make inferences about the causes of behavior or events," and attribution can locate "the cause of an event to factors internal to the person, such as personality traits, moods, attitudes, abilities, or effort" (i.e., an internal attribution) or "external to the person, such as luck, or other people or the situation" (i.e., an external attribution) (p. 127). It is easy to recognize the important role played by the attribution process when the mental health practitioner assesses and treats a client.

The practitioner's personal val-ues, integrated into professionalism, can result in bias. In turn, bias can

> The practitioner's personal values, integrated into professionalism, can result in bias. In turn, bias can evolve to prejudice and discrimination.

evolve to prejudice and discrimination. Affective errors occur because of the practitioner's emotional perception of or reaction to the client, such as liking or disliking. As Groopman (2007) describes it: "Patients and their loved ones swim together with physicians in a sea of feelings. Each needs to keep an eye on a neutral shore where flags are planted to warn of perilous emotional currents" (p. 58). When emotion is involved, the mental health practitioner should guard against a form of self-attribution that Schachter (1964) terms "cognitive-arousal theory." This theory is based on "people do not always know their own feelings" (Fiske, 2004, p. 109), so when the practitioner's attribution to self or to the client is influenced by emotion, there may be inaccurate judgments.

Attribution errors occur when a practitioner assigns negative stereotypes to a client or over generalizes based on socioeconomic, personal, or character factors of the client. For example, seeing service users with similar characteristics (e.g., presenting symptoms) could lead to representativeness error, that is, the practitioner's thinking is shaped and guided by a prototype with only minimum information to match the client to the prototype. Psychological errors may be triggered by the mental health practitioner's failing to collect information, recognize alternatives, or consider possibilities that contradict the prototype, as well as a disproportionate loading of certain prototype-based factors, which leads to a faulty judgments regarding diagnosis and treatment planning.

According to social psychology research, a representative heuristic may be defined as: "A mental shortcut whereby people classify something according to how similar it is to a typical case" (Aronson, Wilson, & Akert, 2007, p. 548). "Representative heuristic is a method of generalization about a given person or target based on partial information or on how closely the exemplar matches the typical or average member of the category" (VandenBos, 2007, p. 790), and thus, "base-rate fallacy a decision-making error in which information about rate of occurrence of some trait in a population (the base-rate information) is ignored or not given proper weight" (p. 103).

ETHICAL CONSIDERATIONS

To be prepared to avoid psychological errors, there should be an understanding of root-cause analysis, error reduction and prevention, and patient safety. Although potentially abstract at first blush, each of these terms has important practical implications.

As for root-cause analysis, VandenBos (2007) defines it as: "A method that identifies the underlying cause or causes of a recurring problem (e.g., in the work place) by using progressively more specific strategies to uncover the source" (p. 805). An error is "a deviation from true or accurate information (e.g., a wrong response or a mistaken belief)" (p. 341), and may be by commission ("an operator performs an incorrect or additional action . . . leading to an inappropriate or duplicate performance of a function" [p. 341]) or by omission ("an operator fails to perform a necessary step or action . . . leading to the failure of a function" [pp. 341–342]). Error reduction requires lessening the "rate at which errors are made" (p. 342).

It is an ethical fundamental (with strong legal consequences) that mental health practitioners must do no harm. There are relevant statements in the ethics codes for the various mental health disciplines. Although the language may differ a bit, there are far more similarities than differences on the issue of doing no harm.

For simplicity and a clear example, I will focus on the language in the code of ethics for psychologists (American Psychological Association, 2002) that directs psychologists to aspire for quality care—of course, the same notion is appropriate for every other mental health discipline. In the APA ethics code, the five General Principles are particularly important for all elements of psychological practice:

Principle A: Beneficience and Nonmaleficence declares "do no harm."
Principle B: Fidelity and Responsibility promotes professional contributions to society and specific communities (including with some pro bono services).
Principle C: Integrity recognizes the importance of accuracy, honesty, and truthfulness.
Principle D: Justice emphasizes fairness and justice for ALL people, and ensuring that psychologists guard against "potential biases, the boundaries of their competence, and the limitations of their expertise do not lead to or condone unjust practices" (p. 1063).
Principle E: Respect for People's Rights and Dignity acknowledges individual rights and the safeguards necessary for protecting "the rights and welfare of persons or communities whose vulnerabilities impair autonomous decision making" (p. 1063). In fact, concern for cultural diversity provides

for an explicit directive: "Psychologists try to eliminate the effect on their work of biases based on those factors, and they do not knowingly participate in or condone activities of others based upon such prejudices" (p. 1063).

Note that integrity is a requisite for quality care, defined as: "the quality of moral consistency, honesty, and truthfulness with oneself and others" (VandenBos, 2007, p. 488). These General Principles, although for psychologists, provide honorable aspirations for any mental health practitioner, regardless of discipline. The actual standards for practice within any mental health discipline will be derived from ethical principles of this nature.

All mental health services are intended to ensure quality care that will protect the service user's safety. Translated into reality, the practitioner must be committed to minimizing or preventing a negative effect or outcome. Although every mental health practitioner will presumably strive to avoid negative effects, Fisher (2009) states: "Recognizing that harms are not always avoidable or inappropriate, Standard 3.04 requires psychologists to take reasonable steps to avoid harming those with whom they interact in their professional and scientific roles and to minimize harm where it is foreseeable and unavoidable" (p. 96). In other words, the filter should be taking reasonable steps to minimize adverse effects from foreseeable and unavoidable errors.

Personal values and beliefs must be compatible with the standards accepted by a profession. Indeed, the definition of a "profession" is predicated on the principle that those who are granted the privilege of being deemed a professional will seek to contribute to the development of society via ethical conduct. Consequently, it is common for a professional association to promulgate a code of ethics, such as from the American Counseling Association (ACA, 2005), American Association for Marriage and Family Therapy (AAMFT, 2001), APA (2002), and National Association of Social Workers (NASW, 1999).

Ethics are steeped in morality, and are devoted to positive conditions. Johnson and Ridley (2008) say: "Ethics—sometimes called moral philosophy—is the branch of philosophy concerned with how we ought to live. Ethics involves establishing principles of right behavior that can be translated to life and work" and an ethics code is limited, albeit considered "necessary but not sufficient" (p. xvi). Personal values and beliefs are enveloped by virtue (moral excellence) and underlie professional ethics.

Preventing psychological errors requires adhering to professional ethics. When providing services, the mental health practitioner should consider whether a communication or event is linked to the relevant discipline, seems to be (even partially) professional in nature, has the potential to affect a service user, and threatens professionalism of the discipline or the practitioner (Pipes, Holstein, & Aguirre, 2005).

Discussing the teaching of ethical behavior, Sternberg (2009) urges defining problematic events as having an ethical dimension, considering its significance, and taking responsibility for generating an ethical solution. The next step involves deciding on what abstract ethical rules might be applicable, and how to apply them to suggest a concrete solution. It will be necessary to guard against contextual forces that might lead to unethical conduct. Then action should occur.

When scrutinizing services and events for possible implications for psychological error, the mental health practitioner should identify the relevant ethical principles and rationally evaluate the alternatives for action. As suggested earlier, values enter into the professional's mental processing of information.

Value-based ethics are defined by virtuous deliberations, emphasizing personal connections and protection of others (i.e., do no harm). Murdick, Gartin, and Crabtree (2007) describe principle-based and value-based ethics. Derived from utilitarianism, principle-based ethics maximize the good. For avoiding psychological errors, they note that: "Three examples of where ethical abandonment might occur are when (a) practical wisdom dictates a different response, (b) shared community values conflict with the proposed action (a form of communitarian ethical theory), or (c) a caring relationship, such as friendship, love, or family, impacts the individual's proposed actions" (p. 245). In other words, ethics may be set aside by personal and community idiosyncrasies. Whether the outcome is acceptable to professionalism is subject to conjecture.

Given that mental health practitioners work with people with abnormalities as well as normalities, the Code of Ethics for Educators of Persons with Exceptionalities (Council for Exceptional Children, 1998) provides some very useful guidelines. Although intended for special education professionals, every tenet presented is applicable to mental health practitioners as well. From an ethical perspective, special educators:

1. Are committed to developing the highest educational and quality of life potential of individuals with exceptionalities.
2. Promote and maintain a high level of competence and integrity to practicing their profession.
3. Engage in professional activities that benefit individuals with exceptionalities, their families, other colleagues, students, or research subjects.
4. Exercise objective professional judgment in the practice of their profession.
5. Strive to advance their knowledge and skills regarding the education of individuals with exceptionalities.
6. Work within the standards and policies of their profession.
7. Seek to uphold and improve where necessary the laws, regulations, and policies governing the delivery of special education and related services and the practice of their profession.
8. Do not condone or participate in unethical or illegal acts, nor violate professional standards. . . . (Council for Exceptional Children, 1998, p. 1)

I believe that, if these ethical principles are maintained, the risk of psychological errors would be reduced markedly.

CLINICAL VERSUS STATISTICAL JUDGMENTS

Earlier mention was made of evidence- and empirically-based practices, approaches that rely on information or data for making decisions for professional services. Notwithstanding evidence or empirical data, in every instance, there is a personal judgment. In order to minimize subjectivity and maximize objectivity, consideration must be given to clinical versus statistical judgments.

> *Notwithstanding evidence or empirical data, in every instance, there is a personal judgment. In order to minimize subjectivity and maximize objectivity, consideration must be given to clinical versus statistical judgments.*

The basis for the clinical versus statistical (or actuarial) controversy is introduced by Matarazzo (1990):

> Rather than being totally objective, assessment involves a subjective component. Specifically, it is the activity of a licensed professional, an artisan familiar with the accumulated findings of his or her young science, who in each instance uses

23

tests, techniques, and a strategy that, whereas also identifying possible deficits, maximizes the chances of discovering each client's full ability and true potential. (p. 1000)

The debate came to the forefront when Meehl (1956) issued his call, "Wanted—A good cookbook," and assailed time-honored views, especially from psychoanalytically oriented theory (Meehl, 1954). For example, he maligned the idea of distinguished Gordon Allport that "psychological causation is always personal and never actuarial" (Allport, 1942, p. 157).

There is a clear-cut difference between decision making in mental health services that is "clinical" versus "statistical." Wierzbicki (1993) offers the following distinctions:

The clinical method involves learning as much as one can about the individual, constructing some abstract model to explain the individual's psychological functioning, and using this model to derive predictions concerning the individual's future functioning (e.g., response to one treatment versus another, likelihood of becoming violent). . . .

The statistical method, on the other hand, involves classifying the individual among similar cases. Empirical techniques are then used to determine how this class of similar cases has behaved in the past. Then, it is assumed that the case in point will behave similarly to members of the comparison group, and so a prediction is derived for the individual which is based on the group's behavior. (p. 131)

The clinical method is idiographic (principles of individuality), whereas the statistical or actuarial approach is nomothetic (ideas that are thought to apply to all persons or make comparisons of the individual to groups of people). Since Meehl's (1954) book *Clinical vs. Statistical Prediction*, there has been great debate and research about the two viewpoints:

Fifty years after Meehl's classic treatise, the evidence is even more clear that informal methods of aggregating data are unlikely to predict behavior as well as formal, actuarial methods when a domain of research is sufficiently advanced as to permit identification and reliable measurement of key variables useful for prediction. (Westen & Weinberger, 2004, p. 609)

To the contrary, Chwalisz (2006) concludes:

It is interesting that statistical and clinical approaches were equally effective in describing and labeling phenomena. Both performed comparably in terms of performing diagnosis, detecting brain impairment, describing personality characteristics, and predicting length of treatment or hospitalization. (p. 392)

She believes that a statistical approach is a useful adjunct to clinical judgment, "especially where bias may impact professional decisions and when those decisions have serious implications (e.g., predicting suicide, predicting violence" (p. 397).

With the passage of time, there has been a significant shift away from the clinical/subjective approach. It seems true that, when cognitively processing information, even the most well-trained mental health practitioner will be influenced at all times by emotion, which can be a harbinger of bias: "We cannot escape the subjectivity of the observer—that we will never see the world exactly as it is" (Westen & Weinberger, 2004, p. 610).

The contemporary preference in the mental health disciplines seems to be reliance on evidence or empirical data—of course the definition of "evidence" and "empirical data" can vary and sometimes be ambiguous. Failing to collect information, to recognize alternatives, or to consider possibilities that contradict the prototype, as well as a disproportionate loading of certain prototype-based factors, may lead to faulty judgments. Therefore, for risk management (i.e., to avoid a disciplinary judgment by a licensing source) the modern mental health practitioner should seek to ensure that clinical judgments have an objective basis.

Prevailing standards support that all judgments in mental health services should be evidence based. This assertion is supported by professional ethics; the APA (2002) ethics code states: "Psychologists' work is based upon established scientific and professional knowledge of the discipline" (Standard 2.04 Bases for Scientific and Professional Judgments, p. 1064).

The commitment to "basing clinical practice on robust, primarily research-based evidence" led to "empirically supported treatments (EST), empirically supported relationships (ESR), evidence-based practices (EBPs), and called for the approval of assorted practice guidelines that are focused on diagnostic categories or behavioral symptoms" (Koocher & Keith-Spiegel, 2008, p. 104). The APA Presidential Task Force on Evidence-Based Practice (2006) gave authoritative support for this framework. Although certain other mental health disciplines may not have moved toward evidence-based and empirically based practices as much as psychology, I believe that contemporary public policies and laws support this as the framework of choice for all current mental health services.

CONCLUSION

Dimidjian and Hollon (2010) recommend "establishing independent systems for monitoring untoward events in clinical practice, reporting descriptive case studies and qualitative research, and making full use of randomized clinical trials, including examining potential active ingredients, mechanisms, moderators, and a broad range of outcomes measured over time . . . treatments fail patients and not the other way around" (p. 31). Barlow (2010) acknowledges a need to refine methods to detect when harm might occur and recommends collaboration between clinicians and scientists. They are advocating strongly that to avoid harm mental health services must be predicated on behavioral science. For trainees and experienced practitioners, it will be necessary for education and training to promote the dissemination and implementation of behavioral science and help mental health professionals skillfully blend the evidence into services (McHugh & Barlow, 2010). As Castonguay et al. (2010) point out, "the task of building such training programs is dictated by psychotherapists' first ethical responsibility to do no harm," and should focus on the "four components of effective training (instruction, modeling, practice, and feedback), as well as on relevant contributions of basic research" (p. 46).

The modern message is unequivocal. To minimize risks that can lead to psychological errors, mental health services must be based on scholarly subject matter and research evidence.

As discussed previously, deficient professional services can occur by omission or commission. Regardless of professional discipline, the mental health practitioner should implement safeguards against "psychological errors." This strategy benefits both quality care and risk management.

The practitioner needs to stay up to date about what a substantial portion of like professionals believes is appropriate or correct for particular services. This requires adequate scholarly knowledge derived from empirical- and evidence-based information.

Social psychology supports the idea that human behavior is strongly influenced by values, beliefs, and biases. The practitioner is not immune from these same influences when making professional judgments, thus, consideration should be given to maximizing objectivity in analyses and decisions about professional services. For example, root cause analysis should preface an intervention; without knowing the causative influences for the problems and regardless of theoretical preferences, there is the possibility of limited efficacy and elevated risks.

The mental health practitioner must strive to do no harm. Being a professional entails a focus on ethics while always promoting contributions to society in general and all service recipients in particular.

THREE

Knowing the Opposition

As a backdrop for evidence-based quality care and risk management, it is necessary to recognize a conundrum. Mental health practitioners deal with real-world problems, but do so within a framework of professionalism. Being a professional practitioner is a "privilege" (not a "right") as defined and granted by society.

A profession is "a business . . . that one publicly avows" (Simpson & Weiner, 1989, p. 572). It is

> a calling requiring specialized knowledge and often long and intensive preparation including instruction in skills and methods as well as in the scientific, historical, or scholarly principles underlying such skills and methods, maintaining by force of organization or concerted opinion high standards of achievement and conduct, and committing its members to continued study and to a kind of work which has for its prime purpose the rendering of public service. (Gove, 1961, p. 1811)

Benjamin (2007) succinctly defines a profession as "specialized knowledge involving intensive training; high standards of practice, usually supported by a code of ethics; continuing education so that practitioners stay current with the latest developments in the profession; and provision of a service to the public" (p. 155).

These definitions show that in order for a mental health practitioner to be admitted into and remain a member of the profession, the mental health practitioner must give emphasis to scholarship and skills and provide services that "are consistent with professional standards and increase the likelihood of desired outcomes" (VandenBos, 2007, p. 763). Risk management is intended to protect all concerned. The "risk" is that consumers and authoritative sources will consider the professional services to be inadequate, inappropriate, or negligent.

Professional standards for mental health services have commonly required scientific information, albeit there may be thoughtful scholarship that is not derived from empirical research per se. Using the discipline of psychology as an example, when the American Psychological Association (APA) was founded, there was a commitment to the "advancement of psychology as a science" (Sokal, 1992, p. 115). Science should undergird the empirical or evidence information upon which a practitioner bases and provides services.

The conundrum arises from the fact that the clinical efforts of practitioners are rewarded with social status and financial revenues. Regrettably, some practitioners tend to give priority to self-rewards and/ or fail to maintain the requisite standards (Dingfelder, 2010)—and society must remedy the faulty situation.

Historically, society called on members of the professional discipline to define, monitor, and control for maintenance of standards. As will be discussed throughout this book, the foregoing functions have now been assigned to other sources, particularly to government, along with the legal system and third-party payment sources. At present, the professional discipline often is subservient to these regulators.

Also in earlier days, the therapeutic alliance between the mental health practitioner and a patient was sacrosanct. Times have changed. The professional relationship, including the hallowed therapeutic alliance, has new members or participants, namely the government and third-party payment sources.

In the mid-1970s, mental health practitioners, especially psychologists (albeit the other disciplines eventually did the same), started zealously pursuing governmental licensing and eligibility for third-party payments (e.g., insurance coverage for mental health services). The other unstated reason was that the mental health practitioners wanted to increase their revenues. In no way should that be viewed as a negative. Certainly the amount of time and money invested in acquiring advanced education and training justifies adequate

Also in earlier days, the therapeutic alliance between the mental health practitioner and a patient was sacrosanct. Times have changed.

financial compensation. For the professional relationship, the message is simply that when another source gets involved, such as a government agency responsible for protecting consumers through licensing or a health insurance company paying for services, there is a *quid pro quo*—the mental health discipline must relinquish control of the profession.

Another significant change in the 1970s was a greater acceptance by society of seeking mental health treatment. As a result, if there were a seemingly legal cause of action, consumers were more willing to "go public" and file a lawsuit against health care practitioners.

In earlier years, mental health patients were reluctant to openly admit that they had received professional services for psychological and behavioral problems. This openness was encouraged by the emergence of community mental health programs that were created by the Comprehensive Community Mental Health Centers Act of 1963. In other words, mental health services became a highly visible part of society and the stigma of having been a patient or client of a mental health practitioner was lessened. With "outside" sources (e.g., governmental licensing boards and health insurance companies) now figuratively in the treatment room as well, there was less reluctance to seek legal redress against alleged negligence, by omission or commission, from a mental health practitioner. Said simply, the doors of the courthouse were thrown open to lawsuits against mental health practitioners.

REDEFINING PATIENTS AND CLIENTS

Another way of conceptualizing the new era of accountability is to consider the reasons why patients and clients became empowered. They paid for their insurance coverage and logically expected quality care. If there was unsatisfactory service, either real or conjured up in the mind of the recipient, legal action could be considered a remedy. If the problem could not be dealt with by a legal action (e.g., the possibility of collecting financial damages was too remote to entice an attorney to take the case on a contingency fee arrangement [percentage of what is collected]), the service user could look to government regulators, such as a licensing board. Filing a complaint to a licensing board (at no financial cost to the complainant) potentially would trigger a prosecutorial evaluation of the licensed practitioner's performance (as discussed in Chapter One). It was reasoned that, if a licensing board administers discipline to a mental health practitioner, a trial attorney might be convinced to file a separate malpractice action (or wrest a settlement from the malpractice insurance carrier).

As mental health practitioners were gaining entry into the Health Care Industry (with its status and financial rewards), the empowerment of patients and clients increased. Historically, the term "patient" suggested an "illness" or "pathology." The term "client" emerged in rejection of the medical model, and was a polite way of saying the person was relying on professional services. The advent of governmental licensing and third-party payments presented a new framework that redefined patients and clients as being "consumers" or "service users."

In the current era, if a person has contact or communicates with a mental health practitioner with a reasonable belief that the encounter or exchange is professional in nature, the person may have acquired the status of service user. In other words, traditional or conventional formalities of developing a professional relationship may not be necessary to impose professional responsibilities and duties on the licensed mental health practitioner. There may, of course, be some differences between jurisdictions on this issue, and the relevant standards for one mental health discipline may be somewhat different from another discipline. Therefore, it is important for the mental health practitioner to obtain consultation regarding these standards of professional responsibility from a qualified attorney. Relying on a colleague for advice may end up being a "blind leading the blind" situation and not adequately inform the practitioner. Obtaining legal counsel

Because professional mental health services came into existence more than a century ago, there has been a steady evolution of the relationship between practitioners and their service users. Today, the treatment alliance between service users and practitioners that existed for the past fifty years has been altered greatly by governmental agencies (via regulatory law) and third-party payment sources.

is an essential "cost of doing business" in today's mental health market-place (Woody, 2008).

Because professional mental health services came into existence more than a century ago, there has been a steady evolution of the relationship between practitioners and their service users. Today, the treatment alliance between service users and practitioners that existed for the past fifty years has been altered greatly by governmental agencies (via regulatory law) and third-party payment sources. This is an era in which respect for the mental health practitioner has been diminished, and new threats to the practitioner's personal rights and safety are commonplace.

SOCIAL AND CULTURAL CONDITIONS

A number of societal and cultural conditions have contributed to the fact that service users today often pose unprecedented and often unjustified risks to the mental health practitioner's rights, safety, and professional practices. In addition to other non-violent risks, data from the Bureau of Labor Statistics identify mental health professionals as having one of the highest rates of workplace violence (Bartol & Bartol, 2012). (Risks from threatening service users will be more fully discussed in Chapter Eight.)

The mental health professions have a long history of expecting and demanding that practitioners always communicate and convey benevolence, nurturance, and altruism to service users. The academic world and professional associations for mental health practitioners promulgated the notion, ethics, and standards that the needs of service users come before any need of the practitioner.

Recently, in a personal discussion about service users who would not pay agreed-on fees (contrary to a treatment contract) with a psychologist, who pompously calls him-/herself a "nationally known expert in mental health ethics," the psychologist clearly sided with the errant clients stating "No matter what the circumstances, benefits for clients come before the interests of practitioners." This "expert's" comment ignores the fact that abusive clients in the discussion were not honoring the *quid pro quo* nature of professional services (i.e., the practitioner provides services, the service recipient pays for the services and adheres to the clinical, ethical, and legal tenets of the treatment context).

It is not all that unusual for a client to receive reimbursement from a health insurance company for a practitioner's bill, yet refuse to pay the mental health practitioner for the professional services rendered. One practitioner lamented, "What has happened to morals and values in mental health clients?" Of course it must be recognized that clients do not often have impeccable life styles, otherwise there would be less or no need for them to receive mental health services.

> *It is not all that unusual for a client to receive reimbursement from a health insurance company for a practitioner's bill, yet refuse to pay the mental health practitioner for the professional services rendered.*

The justifiable viewpoint is that the rights of the practitioner and the service user should be equal in importance, although the professional also has ethical responsibilities and legal duties. "In all debt collection situations, therapists must be aware of the laws that apply in their jurisdiction and make every effort to behave in a cautious, business like fashion" (Koocher & Keith-Spiegel, 2008, p. 185). By the way, it is well established that when a practitioner attempts to collect an overdue debt, the likelihood is increased that a service user will file a complaint of some sort (Koocher & Keith-Spiegel, 2008; Woody, 1988b, 2000b).

Although it remains true that practitioners must respect the rights, dignity, and needs of the service users in the professional context, there is legal justification allowing the practitioner to define, maintain, and protect his or her personal rights and safety. Defining "context," Bennett et al. (2006) say: "Context refers to the total circumstances under which you are seeing the patient, including the setting of the service (e.g., a solo practice, small group, or institution) and the type of service provided (e.g., treatment or evaluative services)" (p. 12). (Chapter Five deals with the Practice Context.)

Every modern mental health practitioner should cease being a "weaponless policeman" (Woody, 1996) and become properly "armed," figuratively and in some instances, literally, to protect his or her personal rights and safety. (Personal protection against violence will be discussed throughout the subsequent chapters, along with recommendations for constructing a zone of privacy and safety in mental health practice.)

When there is an iota of reason to believe that a service user, past or present, has become an "enemy combatant," the practitioner must immediately and unreservedly go on the defense. Being defensive requires that the practitioner be ready and able to act as a defendant or respondent in an ethical, licensing, or legal (malpractice) situation.

If the service user has been critical or threatening, or is noncompliant with the appropriate individualized service plan, the mental health practitioner should set aside any semblance of professional commitment to the rejecting or hostile service user. This termination of commitment is justified when the service user creates increasing liability for the practitioner by continuing to be critical, threatening, or noncompliant, and is on the cusp of being a complainant or litigant.

Modern society has eliminated considerable public funding for comprehensive mental health services, one reason being the economic downturn. The economy also has forced insurance companies to reduce payments for mental health services. Consequently, many people who are ill suited for outpatient services nonetheless turn to private practitioners. The economy relevant to mental health practice now spawns inconsistent, infrequent, and often inadequate professional services (Woody, 2009a).

As a result, mental health practitioners today face more threatening service users, some of whom are potentially violent (it is an understatement to say that modern society is violence prone). In part, this is seemingly due to the lack of community mental health services, as well as changes in morals, values, and the economy. In other words, people with hostile and violent propensities do not readily have or cannot afford the mental health services that are needed. Related to these negative conditions, some people who need inpatient treatment are resorting to outpatient services—and because of the financial problems of independent practice, some mental health professionals are succumbing to accepting clients who are ill suited for outpatient services. Consequently, every mental health practitioner must be prepared to maintain effective self-protection.

Abuse of mental health practitioners may take many forms, such as, but certainly not limited to, dishonesty (e.g., tactics to avoid paying for services), demanding services that are not the "treatment of choice" according to professional standards, violation of the practitioner's right to privacy, and threats to inflict financial harm (e.g., impuning reputation) or physical injury to the practitioner.

That is, whenever a service user issues a threat or encroaches on the personal rights of the mental health practitioner, the practitioner must have immediate preventive actions and safeguards in place.

ABUSIVE CONDUCT BY SERVICE USERS

Abuse of mental health practitioners may take many forms, such as, but certainly not limited to, dishonesty (e.g., tactics to avoid paying for services), demanding services that are not the "treatment of choice" according to professional standards, violation of the practitioner's right to privacy, and threats to inflict financial harm (e.g., impuning reputation) or physical injury to the practitioner. Real-life examples of these and other possible abusive acts by service users will be presented throughout this book to show how service users have blatantly victimized mental health practitioners.

Some of the stories are almost unbelievable, but regrettably are painfully true. For example, one service user fabricated an identity and received services without paying. The naïve practitioner was aghast, saying, "I was trained to trust everyone, otherwise therapy would not be effective."

PUBLIC POLICY, LAW, AND PROFESSIONALISM

Public policy understands and supports that society requires different types of workers. When a body of workers has progressed from an occupation to a semi-profession to a profession, an economic and service monopoly is allowed. As discussed at the outset of this chapter, achieving and maintaining professional status requires that the professionals accept the requirement of formal education and training; the pursuit and development of knowledge, such as through research; the ideal of service to humanity; and the establishing and monitoring of standards and ethics.

Focusing on the requisite standards and ethics, the professional is designated to be a social trustee, which necessitates a professional ideology that embraces ideals and orientations that will benefit society. Brint (1994) states that the dominant form of professionalism reflects "a commitment to the public welfare and high ethical standards combined with a claim to specialized authority over a limited sphere of formal knowledge" (p. 36). Brint also says:

From the professional associations, it took the idea of regulation by the occupational community in relation to high practice standards. From the justifications of the regulatory state, it took the idea of service in relation to the interests of public safety, convenience, and welfare. (p. 36)

For years, the essential regulation of each of the mental health professions was done by national, state, and local professional associations, which commonly relied on the ethics and standards that colleagues in the profession had promulgated and the disciplinary actions taken by their respective ethics committees. For example, psychology, was, for all intents and purposes, assigned exclusively to the APA, mental health counseling to the American Counseling Association (ACA), social work to the National Association of Social Workers (NASW), marriage and family therapy to the American Association for Marriage and Family Therapy (AAMFT), sex counseling and therapy to the American Association of Sexuality Educators, Counselors and Therapists (AASECT), psychiatry to the American Psychiatric Association (ApA), and so on. Through their trusteeships, these professional associations sought to fulfill the public policy obligations attendant to professionalism, but of course the association's "jurisdiction" for each applied only to its dues-paying membership, which might have been a relatively small portion of the practitioners in the particular mental health discipline.

In the mid-1970s, the malpractice courts sent a message of sorts to the mental health professions that they had failed to adequately protect society. Perhaps nowhere is this more evident than in the case of *Tarasoff v. Regents of the University of California*, 17 Cal. 3d. 358, 1976. The *Tarasoff* court rebuked the notion that the tenets of therapy required that services be vested with absolute confidentiality, saying: "In this risk-infested society we can hardly tolerate the further exposure to danger that would result from a concealed knowledge of the therapist that his patient was lethal" (p. 442).

> *For years, the essential regulation of each of the mental health professions was done by national, state, and local professional associations, which commonly relied on the ethics and standards that colleagues in the profession had promulgated and the disciplinary actions taken by their respective ethics committees.*

From the mid-1970s on, the number of malpractice cases against mental health practitioners escalated (Woody, 1988a, 1988b). Reaves and Ogloff (1996) state: "The amount of ongoing litigation in the United States has reached appalling proportions. . . . Although many people seem to abhor this growing trend, the fact remains unaltered" (p. 117). No mental health practitioner is assuredly exempt from the risk of a legal action, yet there is an unhealthy denial. Too often, practitioners "think that others might be accused of ethics violations, but not themselves" (Chauvin & Remley, 1996, p. 563).

Incidentally, it seems that the average mental health practitioner who is the subject of a complaint, regardless of type, is well trained and well intentioned, has been in practice for about 20 years, and consider him-/herself to be strongly committed to professional ethics and standards, as well as the laws and administrative rule applicable to the jurisdiction in which he or she practices. In other words, those practitioners receiving any sort of complaint may not be ignorant, sleazy, careless, or nefarious in their services.

Concurrent with the rise in litigation, mental health practitioners were recognizing the possibility of new and greater economic rewards. Believing that elevated professional status would accommodate more ably competing with medicine for third-party payment sources, mental health practitioners doggedly sought licensure. Naively, practitioners did not fully comprehend that licensure would usher in governmental control of the mental health professions.

Contrary to the wishes of many (myself included), the mental health professions are no longer defined or controlled by colleagues within professional associations. Instead, regulatory laws, such as those implemented by licensing boards, are defining and controlling mental health practices.

Derived from statutory authority, state licensing boards are promulgating administrative rules that micromanage mental health practice; these governmental sources establish the ethics and standards that must be maintained by practitioners. In many instances, the ethics and standards are not clearly specified; consequently, the practitioner must engage in deductive reasoning when interpreting the standards. Obviously conjecture can lead to subjective ideas that may or may not be consonant with the preferences of or mandates from governmental regulators, such as prosecuting attorneys and members of the licensing boards.

Today, mental health licensing boards and their concomitant prosecutorial units engage in unprecedented micromanagement. Mental health practitioners no longer have great discretion in deciding what is appropriate for their professional services; for many issues these determinations are made by the state regulatory system with all its foibles. For example, quality and fairness (i.e., due process and equal protection) are jeopardized by political considerations and lack of knowledge of or experience with mental health services. In one state, investigators for a prosecutorial unit report that they usually have approximately one hour of orientation about how to handle complaints against mental health practitioners, yet they exert a lot of power over shaping and selecting the information that is collected for and transmitted to the prosecutorial unit for decision making.

With the advancement of regulatory law, as with malpractice actions, the number of licensing complaints against mental health practitioners has escalated. Reaves and Ogloff (1996) believe that, as compared to civil actions, "license-related cases are far more serious" (p. 117).

> With the advancement of regulatory law, as with malpractice actions, the number of licensing complaints against mental health practitioners has escalated.

One mental health practitioner, who was exonerated and even received financial compensation from a judgment against the licensing board, said: "I had a major loss of income, because nearly all of the lawyers with whom I had dealt as a forensic expert did not hire me for fear that merely being investigated would forever taint my credibility as an expert witness. My income from forensic cases went from 'fairly busy' to near zero for 10 years—and several managed care companies dropped me from their panels and would not readmit me even after I had been exonerated. I paid an expensive price for victory."

At this point in the discussion, there are two important conclusions to make relevant to public policy, law, and professionalism. First, when professional associations were entrusted to safeguard the public, ethics committees failed to satisfactorily fulfill the task; their performance was often perceived by society as favoring professionals over consumers. Because the ethics committees were composed of professional peers, the public viewed the committees as having an "Old Boys Club" or "Old Girls Club" mentality. This may or may not have been realistic. Second, replacing self-regulation with statutory law has revealed that prosecutors for licensing boards have commonly failed in satisfactorily fulfilling their tasks with sensitivity and fairness to the relevant professional tenets; mental health professionals often perceive prosecutorial performances as favoring consumers over practitioners (Peterson, 2001; Williams, 2001). The underlying problem for both self-regulation and regulatory law is the same: unjust, illogical, and destructive inequality (Woody, 1993).

Consider the following twelve examples, which contain paraphrasing of actual situations from various states involving mental health practitioners defending against regulatory complaints. These examples are presented in a sequence that should prove irrefutably that unjust, illogical, and destructive inequality reigns unfettered in regulatory law today.

EXAMPLE ONE: Negative Views of Practitioners

A prosecuting attorney said, "We [the regulatory agency] were able to get 'instant seizure' subpoena power through the legislature because we know that if we merely issued a subpoena for records, the mental health practitioner would change the records. You can't trust mental health practitioners."

EXAMPLE TWO: Applying 20/20 Hindsight

Sometimes the regulators ignore the victimization of practitioners. Numerous times prosecutors for regulatory agencies have said things such as, "I don't care if the complainant is a serial murderer, what I care about is whether the practitioner may have done something wrong." That is, the prosecutors ignore abusive complainants and go on "fishing expeditions" for possible allegations against practitioners. Also ignored is the complexity of the complainant's psychological characteristics and the fact that hindsight is 20/20.

EXAMPLE THREE: Mysterious Investigations

At the investigative stage in one state, mental health practitioners can be required to respond to an investigation without knowing the specific purpose of the investigation or the allegations of wrongdoing. An investigator explained that the practitioner did not have the right to know if it was the practitioner or some unidentified colleague who was the subject of the investigation. Even when the subject of an investigation is known, the mental health practitioner is not entitled to know who filed the complaint until after a finding of probable cause for discipline has been issued. It is an understatement to say that formulating a defense strategy is hampered and difficult!

EXAMPLE FOUR: Personal Biases

Immediately after a licensing board member touted the importance of APA ethics and incorrectly asserted that the APA ethics prohibited a particular type of conduct, an accurate rebuttal from the practitioner's attorney pinpointed that the conduct under investigation was not prohibited by APA ethics. The licensing board member, with known aspirations to be elected to the state legislature, responded emotionally, "I don't care what is in the APA ethics. As long as I am on the board, what I say is a violation will be a violation."

The foregoing narcissistic outburst by a board member occurred in a state where there had been a previous appellate court ruling against the regulatory agency, which held that any standards or ethics from a professional association could not be applied in regulatory cases unless they had been codified in specific terms by statute or administrative rule. Note that Fisher (2009) states: "Adjudicatory decisions based on an ethics code remain vulnerable to overturn on appeal if defendants can argue they had no forewarning that specific behaviors were ethical violations" (p. 21).

EXAMPLE FIVE: Ignoring the Judiciary

Based on a horrendous child custody battle, the prosecutor for the licensing board engaged in innumerable telephone conferences with the complainant-mother, even after the mother's veracity had been impeached in court. Moreover, this zealous prosecutorial search for a scintilla of wrongdoing by the mental health practitioner continued well after the judge in the child custody case submitted written support for the practitioner.

EXAMPLE SIX: Ignoring Statutory Law

A prosecutor, for the licensing board, advocated discipline against a mental health practitioner for having a handgun in his office, which the client had chanced to detect. The practitioner, however, was licensed by state statute to carry a concealed weapon and had been a certified marksman in the military. The practitioner had not brandished the firearm, and the clinic was in a high-crime neighborhood, which had been burglarized multiple times.

One board member opined, "at least the practitioner should tell a patient that he is carrying a gun," even though this statement was counter to the Second Amendment of the U.S. Constitution and the legislative intent of the state statute that authorized the mental health practitioner to have a license for a concealed weapon. The prosecutor quickly asserted vehemently, "There is absolutely no reason for a mental health practitioner to have a gun." Because the prosecutor was known to carry a handgun in her briefcase, this viewpoint is particularly interesting (the prosecutor never told the practitioner that she had a handgun in her briefcase).

The foregoing is just one example; numerous other scenarios that I have encountered suggest that prosecuting attorneys ignore statutory law.

EXAMPLE SEVEN: Going Beyond the Law

A prosecuting attorney acknowledged, "The problem with the licensing board is that they always expect the highest standard of care, when the law supports only a reasonable, not necessarily a perfect, standard of care." This is a reminder of the statement:

> Perfection is not the standard expected in professional practice. No one is perfect, and everyone makes mistakes or errors based on reasonable judgment calls. People cannot avoid mistakes, but a mistake does not necessarily equal negligence. (Koocher & Keith-Spiegel, 2008, p. 475)

Regrettably, even among presumably professional sources, such as members of licensing boards, the judgments made often lack a rational basis and sometimes derive from personal biases, idiosyncrasies, or egotistical motives.

EXAMPLE EIGHT: Denial of Rights to Reasonably Defend

Despite a state law that allows respondents to a disciplinary complaint to have a copy of any and all documents pertaining to the regulatory agency's investigation, a mental health practitioner learned that the prosecutor for the licensing board had withheld certain documents. The prosecutor made a statement in a board meeting claiming that written information had been received from an insurance fraud investigator, but no such information was contained in the documents provided to the defense attorney. When the defense attorney later contacted the insurance fraud investigator and requested information about the alleged communication to the prosecuting attorney, the insurance carrier could not or would not respond, presumably based (to some degree) on the preferences of the prosecutor.

EXAMPLE NINE: Conjuring Up New Allegations

From a transcript of a meeting of a disciplinary subcommittee for the licensing board, the practitioner's attorney learned that investigative materials, including the rebuttal from the practitioner, had been reviewed and the subcommittee found that there was no basis for disciplining the practitioner. Yet, on the spot, based on a document from a complainant who (next to her signature) stated in writing that she refused to notarize the statements as being true (!), the subcommittee conjured up a new allegation and a finding of probable cause for discipline was issued without allowing the practitioner to know about the new allegation or have an opportunity to defend against it. The matter was rectified only after the practitioner's attorney, in a face-to-face meeting with the two attorneys for the licensing board, hand-delivered a copy of the lawsuit that was about to be filed against the licensing board—a quick huddle by the two state attorneys resulted in an immediate rescission.

EXAMPLE TEN: Unjustified Imposition of Known Error

A licensing board found probable cause for discipline, which subsequently was proven to have involved a seemingly clear reversible error for appeal. Although the complaint was closed and *nolle prosequied* (prosecution was stopped), the licensing board refused to seek removal of the erroneous finding of probable cause from the practitioner's permanent record. This correction could be obtained only by taking the matter to a court of law. With a broken spirit, the practitioner decided to let well enough alone, closed his or her practice, moved out of state, and stopped providing mental health services.

EXAMPLE ELEVEN: Imposing an Irrelevant Intervention Theory

An "expert," well-known for advocacy of cognitive-behavioral ideas, was hired to review a licensing complaint against a mental health practitioner. The report from the expert was a diatribe against "any use of psychoanalytic interventions." Obviously the "expert" was not aware of the evidence supporting the efficacy of psychodynamic psychotherapy (Shedler, 2010). Indeed, at a professional meeting a short time later, the expert told a small group (with me in attendance), "I never read professional journals!"

The attorney for the respondent obtained two other independent experts, who accepted that the psychoanalytic intervention by the practitioner was well done and appropriate. The prosecuting attorney and the subcommittee for the licensing board rejected the opposing opinions and, with a flexing of muscle, said in effect: "If you want to appeal the discipline, go ahead, but remember that we are a governmental agency that needs only mere rationality and our expert will soon be president of the state association for that discipline." On appeal to the entire licensing board (and to the credit of the licensing board as a whole), the board rejected the illogic and close-mindedness of the expert, the prosecutor, and the subcommittee, and the case was dismissed. However by then, the practitioner had suffered considerable emotional distress and legal fees. Only time will tell how this faulty regulatory situation will impact on the practitioner's commitment to career, services made available to the public, and referrals from community sources who learn about the protracted and contested complaint process (which is public record!).

EXAMPLE TWELVE: Denial of Constitutional Rights

Finally, as the *coup de grâce*, there have been many (yes, many) instances in which the mental health practitioner faced with a licensing complaint, more often than not, is treated in a "guilty until proven innocent" manner. In fact, numerous prosecuting attorneys and board members have openly acknowledged this unconstitutional mindset. Moreover, review of the preceding examples reveals jeopardy to Constitutional rights!

THE CAUSE OF UNEQUAL TREATMENT FOR MENTAL HEALTH PRACTITIONERS

In many ways, the fundamental cause of the imbalance in regulatory law is due to the accrual of personal benefits to those in authority. Personal benefits come to the committee and board members, and prosecuting attorneys from satisfying the expectations of governing bodies. Political correctness often permeates modern ethics committees and regulatory agencies.

Several members on licensing boards have told me, "Upon becoming a board member, I found myself being highly skeptical of the members of my profession"; and "Since I was appointed by the governor, I constantly focus on doing what the governor wants, to represent consumer interests and safeguard the public." Members of professional ethics committees have said the same sort of thing: The ideological framework surrounding the board/committee member requires adherence to political implications, which may be weighted more heavily than professional interests; and not creating controversy, which might reflect badly on the political system that created and maintains the regulatory system (yes, professional associations are inherently political).

On a more personal level, members of ethics committees and licensing boards (and the attorneys and administrative staff who provide assistance) have acknowledged that they consciously act according to what will bring them the most favor from their overseers or constituencies. For example, numerous prosecutors and administrative staff for licensing boards have unabashedly acknowledged, "Let's face it, I get promoted, receive a salary increase, and keep my job through prosecuting and winning cases, not dismissing cases."

Understandably, almost everyone in the regulation of the mental health professions seeks a favorable annual review of job performance, as well as the rewards that go along with it (e.g., gaining an appointment to a better role or job). With all due respect, I assert that there are all sorts of violations by omission and commission made by those operating the regulatory system, and that government sources frequently are trampling on the Constitutional rights of the licensee.

Frankly, there seems to be no doubt that only a court of law, with its strict adherence to statutes and rules, will be most likely to ensure a mental health practitioner of equality and fairness, such as (but not limited to) due process and equal protection. However, because mental health practitioners are not trained to be "fighters," the prevailing tendency is often to "throw in the towel" without seeking legal review by a court of law.

The current imbalance between mental health practitioners and their service users is not totally attributable to shortcomings in the ethical or licensing sources. The mental health professions have contributed to the dominance by regulatory law, and allowed the imbalance to develop and continue. In point of fact, the past does not reveal effective self-regulation by the professions. Too often, as mentioned earlier, an "Old Boys Club" or "Old Girls Club" mentality was perceived by the public and was (occasionally? frequently?) present, especially in ethics committees, and there were inadequate protections provided to the public. However, two wrongs do not make a right.

The unbalanced regulatory system is not going completely unnoticed. State legislators do not uniformly support maltreatment of mental health practitioners. One state board, being scrutinized by the legislature, was described as follows: "At this time they [the Board] operate as a star chamber, exempted from public scrutiny, its members are not required to account for their actions" (Cernozubov-Digman, 1997, p. 5).

Is the foregoing description an exaggeration, a universal truth, or applicable to only a few ethics committees or licensing boards? The answer remains for conjecture and personal opinion. What is prudent to assert is that, to date, mental health practitioners have been ineffective in correcting any imbalance.

Despite a professed intention to help improve the situation after a complaint case has been resolved, very few practitioners follow through with any effort to bring about improvements in the regulatory system. Even if the complaint is dismissed, most mental health practitioners believe that revealing that they were investigated will lead to their being judged to be wrongdoers or of questionable competency by other professionals and community sources; recall the comment by Welch (2010), "psychologists are one angry patient, parent or spouse away from professional ruin" (p. 15).

I suspect that it is reasonable to believe that simply defending against a complaint, even if fully exonerated, will produce negative effects for the practitioner. Despite their emphasis on integrity and confidentiality, some mental health professionals engage in gossip, sensationalizing or distorting incidents involving colleagues; so reluctance to admit to a regulatory investigation is likely prudent and well justified.

The emotional and financial demands of defending against ethics and licensing complaints and entering into advocacy to change the systems are great (Charles, Wilbert, & Kennedy, 1984; Woody, 2009b). Therefore, it is understandable that many mental health practitioners would choose to do nothing. As one survivor said, "I plan to get back to work and let someone else fight the battle." Thinking like a warrior is not cultivated in the mental health professions, that is, practitioners are not prepared for professional self-defense and are, instead, often conditioned to kowtow to service users and regulators.

By definition, it would seem that a professional association would, in fact, advocate the needs of the membership, at least as much as the needs of society are advocated. This has not occurred consistently or adequately. It seems that the previously mentioned self-serving benefits, along with the political correctness and personal rewards, may influence professional associations just as much as they influence the regulatory sources.

WHO WILL COMPLAIN OR POSE A LEGAL CHALLENGE?

While providing legal counsel to mental health practitioners faced with ethics or licensing complaints and legal challenges, I often hear the question: "How could I have detected that this particular past client would eventually file a complaint [or lawsuit] against me?" A lament by the practitioner usually follows: "In hindsight, I should have noticed that no matter how good my services, this client would not have been satisfied." Thus, the answer to the question is simply: The mental health practitioner should watch for telltale signs and be wary of accepting any service user who reveals a propensity for complaining (e.g., blaming others for his or her lot in life).

The mental health practitioner should conduct a careful evaluation of the potential client before agreeing to provide services. When the mental health practitioner determines beforehand that the particular potential service user is likely to benefit from the practitioner's particular competencies, both parties to the professional relationship are well served. That is, there is at least a modicum of assurance that there will be quality of care for the service user and risk management for the mental health practitioner.

To the contrary, many mental health practitioners accept almost anyone who requests services, often adopting this nonselective approach because of the negative economics of today's competitive mental health marketplace. Nonetheless, the prudent mental health practitioner should be cautious and define his or her competency

A practitioner's competence for the given clinical issues and a client's probability of or demonstrated noncompliance are valid reasons for not accepting a would-be service user, as well as for terminating a service user after treatment has begun.

in a conservative manner. It is foolhardy to venture into specialty services for which the practitioner does not have clearly established skills. It is also important to assess whether a potential service user appears likely to collaborate and adhere to the individualized treatment plan. A practitioner's competence for the given clinical issues and a client's probability of or demonstrated noncompliance are valid reasons for not accepting a would-be service user, as well as for terminating a service user after treatment has begun.

There is no scientifically determined set of criteria for screening clients for risk management purposes. That said, Bennett et al. (2006) state:

> High-risk patients include those who are diagnosed with serious personality disorders, have complex PTSD or dissociative identity disorders, report recovered memories of abuse, have been abused as children, present a serious risk to harm themselves or others, are wealthy, or are involved in lawsuits or other legal disputes. . . . Patients with serious personality disorders, such as borderline or narcissistic personality disorders, present special risks for psychologists. The specific diagnosis is less important than the presence of special traits, such as a belief in one's entitlement to special treatment, a pattern of idealization and vilification of others, a pervasive inability to accept objective and constructive feedback, or the use of romantic seduction as a consistent strategy to express affection or closeness. (p. 12)

When hearing this information, numerous mental health practitioners have said, "That pretty much describes my entire set of clients."

Consequently, Brock and Barnard (1999) say: "Risk-free therapy simply does not exist; we only can minimize and manage the risk we create" (p. 199).

When screening potential service users, risk assessment should be tailored to the particular service user, with a balancing of idiographic and nomothetic data. Ideas for forensic assessment are relevant; DeMatteo, Batastini, Foster, and Hunt (2010) suggest:

> (1) using structured professional judgment measures, (2) critically evaluating the role of risk factors in each case, (3) employing an adjunctive anamnestic approach [i.e., emphasizing "the patient's historical account of his or her problem with added material from family and friends" (VandenBos, 2007, p. 51)], (4) using a model to guide data collection and interpretation, and (5) remaining aware of factors that may lead evaluators to over-emphasize or under-emphasize specific risk and protective factors. (p. 367)

In addition, there is logic to the following guideline: Carefully scrutinize each and every potential service user for any trace of narcissism. As is well established, narcissism is inherent to numerous diagnoses, such as several personality disorders, especially those with hysterical, psychopathic, sociopathic, or paranoid features.

As a screening framework for whether a potential service user would be apt to unjustly blame or condemn the mental health practitioner, consider the acronym: CONDEMNS. The practitioner should investigate whether the potential service user shows any of these traits:

C = COMPLAINS about his or her lot in life.
O = OWNING responsibility for self is absent (e.g., blames someone else or bad luck for problems).
N = NARCISSISTIC thought processes or verbalizations.
D = DEFENSIVE behavior in many interactions.
E = EXECUTIVE functions are impaired (e.g., faulty planning and decision making).
M = MONEY is an obsession or constant worry, even if unrealistic.
N = NONCOMPLIANT tendencies show up immediately.
S = SUSPICIOUSNESS is a pattern.

Any of the foregoing characteristics could be a harbinger that the service user might, at some juncture, file an ethics or licensing complaint or pose a legal challenge to the mental health practitioner.

Going further, it seems that there is reason to closely evaluate persons suffering chronic pain, those embroiled in a custody/visitation dispute (Kirkland & Kirkland, 2001; Woody, 2000a), or those experiencing multiple personalities or recovered memories (Knapp & VandeCreek, 1997), as they have a high potential for filing complaints. Additional information on this topic may be found in Woody (2000b).

CONCLUSION

All mental health practitioners should subscribe to and uphold the original rationale for having professions in our society, namely that a benefit will occur by ordaining a sector of workers to acquire advanced formal education and training, and pursue and develop knowledge, such as through research. However, the professionals also must manifest an unrelenting devotion to the ideal of service to humanity; this necessitates effectively establishing and monitoring professional standards and ethics.

To quote "Pogo" or some other learned sage, "We have met the enemy and it is us." To minimize the risk of ethical and licensing complaints and legal challenges, mental health practitioners need to assiduously pursue true professionalism by meticulously applying professional ethics and standards in practice.

The modern mental health practitioner, regardless of discipline, faces an unprecedented degree of professional, legal, and personal risks. To not only survive but also to thrive, mental health practitioners must:

1. Seek to provide quality care, relying heavily on ethics, standards, and law;
2. Require adherence to the intervention or therapeutic plan by recipients of professional mental health services;
3. Define and maintain strict boundaries in professional relationships;
4. Keep a protective framework around their personal lives; and
5. Rely on risk management strategies.

Notice that, instead of the equivocal word "should," there are certain matters that, in these times, the mental health practitioner "must" fulfill via the aforementioned five strategies. Otherwise unjustified and unnecessary jeopardy to the service user and the practitioner will occur.

Because of the scientist-practitioner framework in which mental health services should occur, criticisms and protective strategies should be evidence based. Regardless of academic degree, licensure status, years of experience, or employment/service context, the nature of "professionalism" requires that no professional source should be exempt from constructive criticism.

FOUR

A Protective Shield for Professional Services

Mental health services users and practitioners have personal and legal rights. Interwoven into every issue discussed in this book is the theme that mental health practitioners are justified in being defensive. The humanistic era is passed when the practitioner was expected to set aside personal and legal rights in deference to the service user's preferences. That said, the best defense for the mental health practitioner is to be competent, ethical, and pragmatic according to the tenets of the scientist-practitioner model—basing professional services on scholarly evidence and empirical research.

The cornerstone for professional services is providing quality care to the client, which is why this book emphasizes that the practitioner must provide professional services in a manner that yields benefits to society and the particular service user. There is no professional or legal reason why mental health practitioners must sacrifice their rights, which include justified financial compensation and risk management.

> There is no professional or legal reason why mental health practitioners must sacrifice their rights, which include justified financial compensation and risk management.

This chapter presents four key mandates for achieving a legally safe mental health practice. The practitioner must: (1) develop for each client an individualized treatment plan that draws from the best evidence-based practices; (2) focus on avoiding errors in clinical assessment; (3) maintain comprehensive clinical records, which include individualized treatment planning; and (4) carefully analyze and process conflicts with service users to reach ethical decisions that ensure quality care and risk management. Carrying out each of these four practice mandates should protect the interests of the service user and the mental health practitioner equally.

INDIVIDUALIZED TREATMENT PLANNING

More than 25 years ago, a prosecuting attorney with a state licensing board told me, "As soon as I get the clinical records for a complaint case, the first thing that I do is look for an individualized treatment plan, and then I look for a diagnosis that shows that the practitioner had a clinical roadmap." With the passing years, increased emphasis has been placed on professional services being in accord with a plan that is grounded in scholarly thought. In fact, some jurisdictions include individualized treatment planning as a requirement in statutes and administrative code rules.

Professional services must be determined idiosyncratically, that is, tailored to the particular service user. It is outmoded to believe that significant counseling or therapeutic interventions can begin without assessment of what is needed by and appropriate for the particular service user. Therefore, it is illogical to harbor the idea: "As a therapist, I can just listen to the person, and we will peel the onion one layer at a time." In modern mental health services, interventions should be evidence based, which means collecting an array of information from which an individualized treatment plan will be derived. It is a distinct risk management strategy to base all mental health services on formal treatment planning.

Professional services must be determined idiosyncratically, that is, tailored to the particular service user. It is outmoded to believe that significant counseling or therapeutic interventions can begin without assessment of what is needed by and appropriate for the particular service user.

As for the aforementioned prosecuting attorney's concern about diagnosis, the rationale requires far more than simply having a label.

By relying on knowledge derived from scholarly and research sources, the practitioner's use of a diagnostic label or category is merely a code for analysis of the individual. In other words, there is support for having ideas (clinical hypotheses) about the root cause, current symptoms, and alternative treatment strategies. This approach is the threshold to evidence-based treatment planning.

For example, at the advent of providing services to a client experiencing marital problems, psychosocial, psychometric, and nonpsychometric assessment information will reveal idiosyncratic characteristics and their interactive influences within the family system. The practitioner then can consider intervention alternatives and, with the collaboration of the client, establish an individually tailored treatment plan, which will be subject to modifications as new information emerges during the intervention. By basing individualized treatment planning and diagnosis on a foundation of relevant evidence, mental health practitioners will ensure quality care to service users and provide themselves with critical risk management.

There are six components for treatment planning: (1) collecting information that is useful for determining the needs and characteristics unique to the service user; (2) positing long-term objectives and short-term goals for the professional services; (3) determining and evaluating the evidence for the intervention(s) for the particular client and problem(s); (4) implementing methods and strategies tailored to the individual, followed by monitoring for effectiveness; (5) making modifications in the treatment plan as needed and justified; and (6) conducting follow up after termination.

As a reminder, the term "diagnosis" does not contradict attaching an actual clinical category to the service user. For both conceptualizing treatment and providing information to third-party payment sources, the individualized treatment plan should include a specific diagnosis, such as provided by the most recent edition of the *Diagnostic and Statistical Manual of Mental Disorders* (American Psychiatric Association, 1994) or a description of problems if criteria are not met for a specific disorder.

For individualized treatment planning, positing the initial set of long-term objectives and short-term goals should flow from the

The initial version of an individualized treatment plan (and each version thereafter) should contain objectives and goals that are subject to change, as supported by the monitoring of the effectiveness of the methods and strategies.

information collected. The initial version of an individualized treatment plan (and each version thereafter) should contain objectives and goals that are subject to change, as supported by the monitoring of the effectiveness of the methods and strategies.

After the initial assessment, there should be consideration of the appropriateness of the practitioner for the needs of the particular service user. In other words, is the individualized treatment plan of choice within the competency of the practitioner, or do the needs of the client call for referral or transfer to a different service provider? Supporting the idea of referral, Corley (2010) says, "Thinking through how one is vulnerable with certain types of clients and/or at certain times is important" (p. 43).

Quality care and risk management both benefit from clinical supervision. Regardless of the training and experience of the particular practitioner, arrangements should be made when possible to have supervision from another well-qualified practitioner. Someone who is "on the outside looking in" may bring a degree of objective scrutiny of the plan that could reveal recognized or unrecognized personal biases of the practitioner.

As stated several times, the individualized treatment plan should be constantly appraised for appropriateness and effectiveness, and amendments made periodically.

As an aside, I have heard numerous practitioners say, in effect, "I admit that I am rather set in what I believe is the best way to treat people, but it is suitable to everyone whom I see in my practice." This sort of stance generates concern as to whether certain recognized or unrecognized factors (e.g., to increase one's income) may lead to a standardized, "one size fits all" approach rather than individualized treatment planning. In my opinion, this is both foolhardy and potentially nonprofessional.

Inherent to all of the suggestions for individualized treatment planning is the idea that each and every treatment strategy should be linked to the needs of the particular service user. This suggests that no two treatment plans should be the same. The objectives and goals, the strategies selected, and the qualitative aspects of the treatment context and therapeutic alliance should be unique to the service user. Collaboration between practitioner and the services user is an essential ingredient for crafting an individualized treatment plan. Although this principle would seem basic in professional practice, many complaints against practitioners can be traced to the lack of wise individualized treatment planning.

Risk management justifies the practitioner's requiring the client to adhere to the treatment plan. As part of the *quid pro quo* nature of the professional alliance, the practitioner must provide quality care and the client must adhere to the treatment plan and make payments for service. Noncompliance by the service user should be confronted and recognized as an impediment to treatment effectiveness.

Upon termination of treatment, a closing summary should be prepared and made part of the treatment planning records. In addition, after a period of time relevant to the particular service user, the practitioner should follow up on the effectiveness of the professional services and determine if additional services should be recommended, be it from the practitioner or through referral to another service provider. To forewarn the client of follow-up contacts (and thereby avoid resentment), there should be a predetermined follow-up policy about periodic contacts with former clients.

This discussion of individualized treatment plans is essentially a framework for quality care to benefit the service user and risk management to benefit the service provider (which also offers indirect benefits to the service user). By adhering to individual treatment planning, the mental health practitioner is achieving important protection from any adverse actions later on.

AVOIDING ERRORS IN CLINICAL ASSESSMENT

As mentioned, assessment is essential to individualized treatment planning. Dishion and Stormshak (2007) state: "If there is one practice that would improve the standards of mental health care for children and families, it would be the use of a comprehensive assessment strategy for decision making" (p. 104).

When selecting assessment strategies, the practitioner should consider objectivity, including reliability and validity for each source of information. Some practitioners, especially those who are intervention oriented, tend to eschew psychological assessment methods, such as the use of psychometric instruments. Numerous practitioners have told me that they avoid psychological assessment

When selecting assessment strategies, the practitioner should consider objectivity, including reliability and validity for each source of information.

strategies because of limited financial coverage from third-party payment sources. When quality care is at issue, financial considerations cannot be allowed to dominate professional decision making.

Mental health practitioners must be aware that within the assessment process, test scores may be tainted (Lyman, 1978, 1991). Walsh and Betz (2001) point out five sources of error in test scores:

1. Time influence, "due to fluctuations in test performance over time."
2. The content of the test items, although "selected to be representative of or reflective of the characteristics of interest . . . the items selected represent only a sample of those that could measure the characteristics."
3. Administration/scoring errors, "the test administrator fails to administer the test correctly or if the test is improperly scored."
4. Inconsistent conditions between situations, "conditions are not constant from one situation to the next or if conditions distract the individual from full attention to the testing process."
5. Examinee factors, "sickness or fatigue . . . [and] individuals who aren't motivated to do well" (p. 48).

Some of these possible sources of errors are linked to the competency and diligence of the mental health practitioner, and are not shortcomings of the testing instruments per se.

The possibility of errors arising in testing situations has resulted in professional standards requiring that mental health practitioners provide safeguards. For example, the Florida Board of Psychology recognizes the possibility of errors associated with psychological assessment. Administrative Code Rule 64B19-18.004 addresses the use of test instruments, and warns: "(1) The Board finds that the inappropriate use of test instruments is harmful to consumers."

The psychologist is given specific directions.

> (2) A psychologist who uses test instruments in the psychologist's practice of psychology:
> a. Must consider whether research supports the underlying presumptions that govern the interpretive statements that would be made by the test instruments as a result of its completion by any service user;

    b. Must be able to justify the selection of any particular test instrument for the particular service user who takes the test at the instruction of the psychologist;

    c. Must integrate and reconcile the interpretive statements made by the test instrument based on group norms, with the psychologist's independent professional knowledge, evaluation and assessment of the individual who takes the test; and

    d. Must specify in the test report the name of each person who assisted the psychologist in the administration of the test, and the role which that person played in the administration of the test.

Here again, errors could emerge from psychometric limitations or the competency and due diligence of the mental health practitioner. As a caveat, although this administrative code rule is directed at Florida licensed psychologists, the principles would seem relevant to a mental health practitioner in any professional discipline and in any jurisdiction.

Human nature is such that inadvertence can easily occur in almost any professional strategy, and most certainly in clinical assessment. Lyman (1991) cautions practitioners about mistakes occurring in the administration and scoring of tests, as well as the reporting of results. With commitment to avoiding psychological errors, the practitioner who administers, scores, and interprets psychological tests should:

1. Adhere strictly to the standardized procedures—for administration;
2. Consciously apply the knowledge base relevant to the effort—the points given for a response to a particular test item;
3. Administer with a clear mental focus—attend to and concentrate on the task at hand; and
4. Double-check any conclusion for scholarly and technical appropriateness.

Because of the benefits that accrue for both quality care and risk management, the conscientious mental health practitioner will always be diligent and focused on the task.

Always there must be concern about test construction, especially the possibility of test bias: "the tendency of a test to systematically over- or underestimate the true scores of individuals to whom that test is administered or those who are members of particular groups (e.g., ethnic minorities, sexes, etc.)" (VandenBos, 2007, p. 931). Even the best of objective psychological tests commonly has an error of measurement: "any deviation or departure of a measurement from its true value" (p. 341).

MAINTAINING CLINICAL RECORDS

Written records of what occurs during the mental health service (herein referred to as "clinical records") afford strong protection for quality care to benefit the service user and against later negative actions that might be taken against the practitioner:

> Records may serve as useful roadmaps for treatment, documenting the need for services, the treatment plan, the course of treatment, and the process of termination. Records may ease the process of transition when service recipients must obtain assistance from other providers and may help in resolving disputes regarding such issues as the nature of the provided care, fee arrangements, or the effects of treatment. (Drogin, Connell, Foote, & Sturm, 2010, p. 237)

By legal principle, recordings made contemporaneously to an event are commonly weighted heavily by a judge or jury in a malpractice legal action. For example, if a mental health practitioner wrote a clinical record soon after an intervention session, the burden would shift to the accuser to prove that something otherwise occurred. This is one of the two reasons for preserving clinical records for a number of years: (1) Preserving the clinical records benefits the service user by making the records available to a subsequent treatment source, and (2) the preservation of clinical records benefits the practitioner by being a contemporaneous account of what occurred in a professional context, which could be used for defense purposes years later.

Maintaining ongoing comprehensive clinical records also enhances individualized treatment planning. Writing a record of what happened during each session, including critical or analytic comments, keeps the focus on constructing and understanding meaningful objectives and goals and determining whether strategies are proving to be effective. Clearly record keeping is relevant to monitoring and modifying professional services for both quality care and risk management.

Maintaining ongoing comprehensive clinical records also enhances individualized treatment planning. Writing a record of what happened during each session, including critical or analytic comments, keeps the focus on constructing and understanding meaningful objectives and goals and determining whether strategies are proving to be effective.

Too many mental health practitioners harbor illogical ideas about clinical records. Some practitioners believe that nothing should be included that might be used to the service user's disadvantage, say in litigation. This notion is alien to the purpose of clinical records. Advocating issues beyond clinical objectives and goals is not appropriate for clinical records. Some practitioners think that records should be minimal; this view leaves the practitioner without risk protection and open to criticism for not providing quality care to service users. A few practitioners believe that no clinical records should be kept. By modern standards, keeping minimal or no clinical records portends to be malpractice.

In most, perhaps all, state jurisdictions, statutes or administrative code rules mandate that licensed mental health practitioners keep clinical records, and some jurisdictions impose detailed requirements for what will be in the clinical records and how the records will be safeguarded and preserved. As an example, consider Florida Administrative Code Rule 64B19-19.0025, which states the following mandate: "To serve and protect users of psychological services, the psychologists' records must meet minimum requirements for chronicling and documenting the services performed by the psychologists, documenting informed consent and recording financial transaction." Rule 64B19-19.0025 then goes on to specify what the contents should include:

> Records for chronicling and documenting psychologists'
> services must include the following: basic identification
> data such as name, address, telephone number, age and sex;

presenting symptoms or requests for services; dates of service and types of services provided. Additionally, as applicable these records must include: test data (previous and current); history including relevant medical data and medication, especially current; what transpired during the service sessions; significant actions by the psychologist, service user, and service payers; psychologist's indications suggesting possible sensitive matters like threats; progress notes; copies of correspondence related to assessment or services provided; and notes concerning relevant psychologist's conversation with persons significant to the service user.

By federal law, the Health Insurance Portability and Accountability Act (HIPAA) sets forth a myriad of legal requirements regarding clinical records (Zuckerman, 2006). HIPAA is intended to benefit patients, such as safeguarding privacy. Any prescriptions or proscriptions within the federal laws or the state jurisdiction of the mental health practitioner must be honored fully.

When a complaint of any kind is filed, the investigator or opposing counsel expects to receive comprehensive clinical records from the service provider. Any lack of or faulty record keeping is likely to strengthen the allegations of wrongdoing, therefore, clinical records give the mental health practitioner valuable protection.

To better understand the importance of clinical records for quality care and risk management, Robertson and Woody (1997) recommend that the mental health practitioner continually analyze a service user's records. The on-going analysis serves the following purposes:

(1) gaining an understanding of the influences (positive and negative) in the client's psychological makeup; (2) identifying any special considerations; (3) evaluating the findings of other assessment data sources; (4) weighing the efficacy of past interventions (i.e., how successful or unsuccessful they have been); and (5) formulating a psychodiagnostic preface for the client that will allow subsequent assessment strategies and other interventions to be optimally beneficial and efficient. (pp. 101–102)

Clinical records (a) advise other service providers, such as practitioners who treat a service user in the future, about information that will enhance the quality of the care; (b) document what did and did not occur in the professional context, as would be helpful for risk management (e.g., defending against complaints); and (c) provide for an analysis of services, revealing any potential sources for errors. (Chapter Two explained psychological errors and offered ideas about preventing them.) From review of the clinical records, the practitioner can accommodate the service user's treatment needs, justify amendments to the treatment plan, correct errors, and create a more effective course of action. To summarize, the clinical records should reflect the practitioner's evaluation strategies and use of the information in decision making.

A final point relevant to maintaining clinical records pertains to the source of the information. In the context of collecting information for individualized treatment planning and the preparation of clinical records, the prudent mental health practitioner will need to be mindful of the credibility of the source of information.

An information source may or may not be attempting to purposefully mislead the mental health practitioner. Human nature may lead a person to acquiescence (Lanyon & Goodstein, 1997), producing what is believed to be socially desirable information (i.e., what the practitioner wants to hear). For example, an information source may, perhaps because of the professional status of the practitioner, reflect acquiescence, "a tendency to agree more than disagree" (Domino, 2000, p. 465). Social desirability can lead to both faking good and faking bad, depending on the context of the psychological assessment, that is, the purpose and potential consequences for the information source.

The information source may want to create a negative impression (i.e., a "negative response bias"), such as describing self or others as being "more impaired, sick, or disabled than one actually is" (Boyd, McLearen, Meyer, & Denney, 2007, p. 1). Conversely, the information source may wish to create a positive impression, such as exaggerating positive traits. In certain types of situations (e.g., a forensic context, a child custody evaluation) "a subject may engage in denial of negative traits, or enhancement of positive traits, or both types of deceptions" (p. 14). The clinical records should reflect the practitioner's assessment of outside information and the basis for decision making within the assessment process.

ETHICS-BASED DECISION MAKING

The mental health practitioner's chosen response to a client commonly is by pattern recognition. The observables—test data, nonverbal cues, language—all allow the experienced clinician to take shortcuts (i.e., heuristics), such as developing hypotheses from limited information. Highly common in clinical diagnoses, heuristics lead to fast and frugal decision making.

From the outset, the practitioner may mull over a select set of possible diagnoses in rapid-fire fashion. For the practitioner who has had solid training and enriching experiences, pattern recognition does not necessarily result in a higher incidence of errors, but for less competent clinicians, the use of pattern recognition can result in drastic misjudgments. In all stages of professional services, decision making should not be rushed.

Being focused in the decision making process can lead to productive anxiety, which allows the diagnostician to achieve a level of tension and anxiety that is optimal for forming sharp opinions in an expeditious manner. The application of professional ethics is an important safeguard for decision making, whether for individualized treatment planning, clinical assessment, or information for inclusion in the clinical records.

> *The application of professional ethics is an important safeguard for decision making, whether for individualized treatment planning, clinical assessment, or information for inclusion in the clinical records.*

Whenever a dilemma arises, the mental health practitioner should rely on ethical principles and standards and engage in problem solving. The mental health practitioner should: (1) identify and define the problem; (2) use ethics for engaging in analysis and giving consideration to seeming relevant and material bits of information; (3) search for and develop alternative ways to deal with the problem; (4) choose what seems to be the best solution (with knowledge that another solution may need to be tried); and (5) convert the problem solving into actions (monitoring for effectiveness) (Drucker, 1974).

According to Koocher and Keith-Spiegel (2008), there should be a nine-step ethical decision making strategy in mental health services. The practitioner should:

1. "Determine whether the matter truly involves ethics" (p. 21).
2. "Consult guidelines already available that might apply to a possible mechanism for resolution" (p. 21).
3. "Pause to consider, as best as possible, all factors that might influence the decision you will make" (p. 22)
4. "Consult with a trusted colleague" (p. 22).
5. "Evaluate the rights, responsibilities, and vulnerability of all affected parties, including, if relevant, an institution and the general public" (p. 23).
6. "Generate alternative decisions" (p. 23).
7. "Enumerate the consequences of making each decision" (p. 23).
8. "Make the decision" (p. 23).
9. "Implement the decision" (p. 24).

Decision making for solving problems is a dynamic process. It will not be necessarily a one-time occurrence. Indeed, it is best to continually seek to enhance the solutions, because seldom will there be a single solution to any problem.

This dynamic process has been called an "action cycle," which has numerous aspects of decision making occurring simultaneously. Hoy and Miskel (1996) suggest five steps:

1. The problem should be conceptualized (defined), guarding against a seemingly simple problem that masks a more complex situation.
2. There should be a focus on difficulties (analysis) that are present that will allow for insight-creating ideas.
3. Criteria for problem resolutions should be specified, as will allow judging or evaluating possible alternatives.
4. A distinct plan of action should be chosen.
5. The seeming action of choice should be implemented.

To apply these five steps to a scenario, consider parents who are at odds over how to guide and discipline their children. First, descriptions of recognized emotional and behavior difficulties would be elicited from all members of the family. Second, the practitioner would help all family members in identifying and owning their individual contribution to the problems. Third, there would be collaborative efforts to pinpoint what has been tried for problem solving, the outcomes (degree of success or failure), and what alternatives remain to be tried. Fourth, specific recommendations would be made, accommodating each individual's capabilities, motivations, and defenses. Fifth, the family members would interact according to the agreed on action plan, monitoring what happened and reporting back in the next session. Then the five-step sequence could start again.

The point of a systematic ethical decision making process for mental health services is to prevent faulty judgments. The consequences include prevention of psychological errors, which enhances quality care and provides risk management.

In keeping with prevention of psychological errors, ethical analysis and decision making should be proactive—made before the problem occurs. Koocher and Keith-Spiegel (2008) comment: "The ideal resolution results when a decision can be made *prior* to the commission of an ethical infraction that would otherwise have untoward consequences" (p. 23).

Decision making based on ethics accepts that psychological errors result from faulty reasoning and judgment, with very few psychological errors occurring because of lack of academic knowledge (i.e., not thinking clearly about the available information) (Groopman, 2007). It is important to base decisions on the client's unique story. Decision making should consider: (1) individual strengths and weaknesses; (2) needs and characteristics; and (3) available resources. The practitioner's cognitions or thoughts must be: (1) academically based; (2) free from impairment; and (3) consonant with ethics, standards, and laws pertaining to mental health services.

The pragmatic goal for ethical decision making is to minimize subjectivity, and acknowledge its possible influence on any opinion or communication expressed by the psychologist. As an example of the connection between ethics and subjectivity, the APA (2002) ethics code offers specific steps that should reduce subjectivity: "Psychologists document the efforts they made and the results of those efforts, clarify the probable impact of their limited information on the reliability and validity of their opinions, and appropriately limit the nature and extent of their conclusions or recommendations"; and "Psychologists describe the strengths and limitations of test results and interpretation" (p. 1071). These actions present a logical standard for all mental health practitioners.

Consciously engaging in ethical decision making does not ensure perfection, but the goal is to improve the necessary clinical judgments so as to benefit the service user and society. Thorne (1961) states, "even in view of the admitted invalidity or relative inefficiency of many clinical decisions, society must depend upon clinical decisions because of the practical and economic limitations of life situations" (p. 23). The decision making process is directed at minimizing the subjectivity; the practitioner engages in

> . . . a constant search for scientific support and validation . . . the practitioner should only assert that he or she is doing the best that can be: (1) done at this particular point in the societal-professional evolution; and (2) offered under the existing conditions, in the particular contextual framework, and to the specific client being served. (Robertson & Woody, 1997, p. 65)

Any ethical decision made about a solution to a problem should be considered temporary. The mental health practitioner should be prepared to make additional decisions or take other actions if there is a flare up or difficulty. This reality leads to the term "fire fighting," which "refers to making immediate, short-term decisions that provide temporary solutions to superficial problems" (Chance & Chance, 2002, p. 178). An immediate problem can be considered a symptom of a greater problem, and dealing with it may not cure the disease—other, systemically based problems may be forthcoming.

Dealing systemically within one's approach to mental health practice is a major undertaking. It is human nature for a person to resist change and to be close-minded to new ideas, including how to practice mental health services.

Also, as mentioned previously, decisions are influenced greatly by the practitioner's personal qualities. For example, the prevention of psychological errors is often challenged by the fact: "Research tells us that most therapists can formulate what they *should* do. However, they will more likely respond to their own values and practicalities when determining what they would *actually* do, which is less than they know they should do" (Koocher & Keith-Spiegel, 2008, p. 24).

Close-mindedness may be caused by self-doubt and fear of criticisms from others, such as from professional colleagues and service users. One practitioner stood up during a conference and proclaimed, "I don't see any reason why I should have to rely on objective data for clinical decisions, I have been doing cases of this kind for 25 years, I know the correct answers." Obviously this nonprofessional posture reflects the old adage,

"Don't confuse me with the facts" (and reflects potentially detrimental narcissism). Close-mindedness is rooted in doubting competence and reveals a desperate resorting to self-aggrandizement.

In order to be more competent in preventing psychological errors, the mental health practitioner should make a commitment to personal-professional development by "a coherent, systematically planned, sustained effort at self-study and improvement, focusing explicitly on change in formal and informal procedures, processes, norms, or structures, and using behavioral science concepts" (Fullan, Miles, & Taylor, 1980, p. 135). This position argues that every mental health practitioner must constantly maintain and upgrade competence. For example, the APA (2002) code of ethics states: "Psychologists undertake ongoing efforts to develop and maintain their competence" (2.03 Maintaining Competence, p. 1064).

Implementing this guideline implies that change, at times, will be needed. Accomplishing change in the practitioner's approach to mental health services requires the following nine-step plan:

1. Recognizing and accepting that change can be beneficial;
2. Adopting a conscious commitment to change;
3. Deciding what factors or conditions may be jeopardizing or lessening quality performance;
4. Acquiring new knowledge and skills that will have application to points of vulnerability;
5. Being sensitive to and overcoming personal resistances to change;
6. Allowing accomplishments to be reinforcement for continued change and improved performance;
7. Refining strategies for improvements;
8. Stabilizing quality; and
9. Remaining open to continued efforts for even greater achievement.

After progressing through these nine steps, the mental health practitioner should remain open to potentially starting the cycle again. The possibility of change for improved and safe professional practice should be omnipresent.

For ethical reasons, sometimes it may be helpful to enlist the support, reinforcement, and teaching of a colleague, mentor, or supervisor (Castonguay et al., 2010; Corey & Corey, 2007). This person could be deemed a "change agent," and would serve as: (a) catalyst, (b) solution giver, (c) process helper, and (d) resource linker (Havelock, 1973, pp. 8–9). The social interaction with a change agent is, in and of itself, potentially helpful for accomplishing innovations.

It is an ethical concern that, in this age of electronic information processing, many practitioners experience "information overload." The busy mental health practitioner is certainly vulnerable to not being able to process, organize, and store information for retrieval. This deficit could result in faulty clinical and financial records and in omitting critical case management communications needed for motivational and intervention purposes. Chance and Chance (2002) point out that information overload can lead to ignoring certain information (omission), incorrect informational processing (error), delays in processing (queuing), neglect of certain important information (filtering), resorting to generalized responses (approximation), decentralizing communication processes (multiple channels), and escaping from communication tasks (escape). Among communication theories, these reactions to information overload are considered "inherently dysfunctional" (p. 160), although it might be possible for some of these alternatives to be used in a constructive fashion.

CONCLUSION

At the beginning of this chapter, four key mandates for achieving a legally safe mental health practice were set out. It was asserted that the practitioner must: (1) develop an individualized treatment plan for each client that draws on the best evidence-based practices; (2) focus on avoiding errors in clinical assessment; (3) maintain comprehensive clinical records, which encompass individualized treatment planning; and (4) carefully analyze and process conflicts with service users to reach ethical decisions that ensure quality care and risk management. These mandates offer a protective shield for professional services—the service user will benefit from the improved quality of care and the mental health practitioner will be protected from making errors and having to defend against nefarious complaints. It is a win-win situation.

Every mental health practitioner should continually make a conscious effort to prevent any sort of psychological error, and if an error should occur, by inadvertence or otherwise, the practitioner should take immediate and effective remedial action. By appraising the efforts of the practitioner and the results of professional services (acknowledging the strengths and limitations), there is a preventive filter through which the mental health practitioner can pass information for professional decisions. The practitioner's search for the root cause(s) necessitates identifying the influences that contributed to the what, why, when, where, and how certain psychological and behavioral conditions first occurred, as well as motivated the client to implement a request for professional services.

The wisdom and accuracy of the judgments made by the practitioner construct the foundation for professional expertise (aka "clinical acumen"). Error reduction and the prevention of errors are accomplished when the practitioner continually:

- Seeks additional professional training (e.g., as required by the continuing education requirements for renewal of the license to practice in a particular mental health discipline);
- Is committed to open-mindedness (e.g., considers new empirically and evidence-based information) and counteracts close-mindedness (e.g., never harbors the delusion that the "right answer" exists); and
- Avoids (or at least minimizes) subjectivity (e.g., does not rely on personal notions derived from experiences or ignore behavioral science) and pursues objectivity.

Maintaining and improving clinical acumen, open-mindedness, and objectivity should be a career-long objective, albeit challenging. These qualities contribute to a protective shield for the mental health practitioner.

As for "patient safety," careful development and monitoring of the individualized treatment plan is intended to safeguard the patient. A protective shield requires astute treatment planning.

Earlier comments explored the potential for bias, as might occur when a mental health practitioner makes attributions about a service user. Highly common in clinical diagnoses, social heuristics lead to fast and frugal—but potentially faulty—decisions. A select set of possible diagnoses may be mulled over in rapid-fire fashion. If there has been solid training and enriching experiences, pattern recognition does not necessarily result in a higher incidence of errors, but for less competent mental health practitioners, pattern recognition can result in drastic misjudgments.

All mental health services should be based on ethical decisions that are strategically appropriate to the particular service users. As I have said before, a logical (I would opine mandatory) strategy is to have an individualized service or treatment plan, with specific short-term and long-term goals and objectives (subject to revision as needed). A service or treatment plan is compatible with evidence-based professional services, and will promote efficacy (benefits) and help contradict a tendency for treatment bias, that is, "a tendency for a type of treatment given to a patient to be determined or influenced by the social class or cultural background of that patient" (VandenBos, 2007, p. 956).

The issues discussed in this chapter support 12 specific guidelines for creating a protective shield for professional services:

1. The mental health practitioner should not rush decision making when providing mental health services.
2. The mental health practitioner should always stay focused on the processes and dynamics that are present or unfolding.
3. The mental health practitioner should have a degree of anxiety that motivates forming sharp opinions in an expeditious manner.
4. The mental health practitioner should identify sources of relevant and preferably empirically based information, and build a behavioral science basis for the service when making a professional decision or determination of any kind.
5. The mental health practitioner should consider that professional expertise requires ongoing scholarly and personal/professional development.
6. The mental health practitioner should have evidence-based or objective information as the *sine qua non* of every professional mental health service.
7. The mental health practitioner should have interventions that are evidence-based (including, when appropriate, empirical data) and adapted as needed to an individualized treatment plan, regardless of the individual service user's psychological or behavioral needs or the theoretical preferences of the mental health practitioner.
8. The mental health practitioner should have a check-and-balance system (e.g., supervision or consultation) to reduce psychological error created by the subjectivity that is always present in clinical judgments.

9. The mental health practitioner must operate with open-mindedness.
10. The mental health practitioner should carefully screen all new service users for compatibility with his or her existing professional competence.
11. The mental health practitioner should require that the service user collaborate with the practitioner to achieve consistent and strict compliance with the professional policies and standards (e.g., the treatment plan).
12. The mental health practitioner should focus on and implement immediate corrective measures if a psychological error is made, whether by inadvertence or failure to make an adequate assessment or decision.

Even with adherence to these guidelines, psychological errors will still occur, but the protective shield will be helpful for warding off faulty judgments and remedying any errors that cannot be avoided.

FIVE

The Practice Context

Although emphasis on the interpersonal relationships in which a mental health practitioner engages is well deserved, there also must be strong awareness and management of the conditions in which the professional services are extended to service users. This issue involves more than just the attractiveness of the offices. Furnishings, accoutrements, and location are potential influences on the acceptance of the practitioner and services; there also is considerably more influence from the "culture" or "atmosphere" that prevails in and is applied to the "context."

At the threshold, the practitioner's self-awareness and appraisal are influenced by the mere fact that someone else is assessing the aforementioned conditions. Usually scrutiny from others (e.g., service users, third-party payments sources) leads the practitioner to be cautious and hold the line on quality control—which is good.

There are some practitioners, because of personality characteristics, who delude themselves into believing that others will perceive something as being impressive, when, in

> At the threshold, the practitioner's self-awareness and appraisal are influenced by the mere fact that someone else is assessing the aforementioned conditions. Usually scrutiny from others leads the practitioner to be cautious and hold the line on quality control—which is good.

fact, a negative perception is formed. Needless to say, this is not a good thing. Avoiding problems necessitates creating positive impressions, valid opinions, and constructive actions for all who are stakeholders in the enterprise.

One practitioner places great importance on having an office in an up-scale building with designer-level furnishings, extra office personnel (more for appearance than actual need), and fancy promotional materials, along with the practitioner's attire being ultra fashionable. What the practitioner believes is the ultimate in practice behavior and language is, however, often perceived by some services users and professional colleagues in the community as being ostentatious, false erudition, and snobbish narcissism.

In addition to other professionals speaking ill about the practitioner (which obviously impacts negatively on referrals), this practitioner has had in a decade, more conflicts, complaints, and legal disputes with service users than most practitioners encounter in a lifetime. Moreover, due to overspending, the practitioner is reportedly teetering on the brink of bankruptcy.

The morality message is that prudence and conservatism should prevail in the organizational context. In health care services of any kind, there can, of course, be varied "qualities" of the conditions in which the services occur. However, there should be fail-safe techniques for evaluating decision making that determines the conditions and factors inherent in the service delivery systems. Sometimes self-judgment about what is believed to be persuasive or contextual qualities is flawed by too much subjectivity.

The correspondence or similarity between a practitioner's attitudes about professional services and the practitioner's behavior are not necessarily correlated positively. That is, with a lack of authenticity, one can role play (such as the mannerisms evident in relationships with service users and colleagues). R. A. Baron, Byrne, and Branscombe (2006) caution: "When we meet someone for the first time, we usually react to a variety of factors. Any observable cue, no matter how superficial, may evoke a stereotype, and the resulting emotional reactions lead to instant likes and dislikes" (p. 276). The mental health practitioner who does not maintain authenticity and veracity in communications is apt to suffer negative consequences.

For the mental health practitioner to achieve both quality care and risk management, three terms merit discussion: (1) culture, (2) atmosphere, and (3) context. According to Kassin, Fein, and Markus (2011): "Culture may be considered to be a system of enduring meanings, beliefs, values, assumptions, institutions, and practices shared by a large group of people and transmitted from one generation to the next" (p. 19). Atmosphere refers to: "The tendency for particular behaviors to be stimulated by a particular environment or situation, even when inappropriate" (VandenBos, 2007, p. 81). Contextualization is: "The recognition of the role that social and cultural contexts (situations or characteristics) have in shaping human behavior" (Organista, Marin, & Chun, 2010, p. 63).

THE SOCIOCULTURAL CONTEXT

In addition to culture, atmosphere, and context, mental health practitioners are subject to the regulatory influences and controls of the overall (macro) sociocultural context (including the political and governmental systems). Norcross, Freedheim, and VandenBos (2011) say, "Cultural norms and political institutions shape both individual lives and professions' trajectories" (p. 745).

Mental health practice is definitely on the cusp of major contextual changes. Particularly important are the issues of the so-called multicultural revolution (which requires culturally sensitive mental health services) and the reshaping of democracy toward a more socialistic model, that is, a marked increase in government prescriptions and proscriptions for all sorts of health care services. All of these conditions have relevance to financial conditions as well.

This is not the place to debate the wisdom or foolishness of these sociocultural changes for the mental health service context. Because the focus is on preventing legal challenges, it is highly germane to note that the practitioner's success-failure is greatly influenced (some would opine "determined") by the progressive shifts in the sociocultural context.

QUALITY CARE

Beyond the practitioner's competency and professionalism, the contextual cornerstone for safety against legal challenges in mental health practice is, as stated throughout this book, quality care. The practice

There is no justification whatsoever for allowing a practitioner to avoid or denigrate professional standards and ethics or state and federal laws relevant to clinical and business records. As with client management, operational policies provide benefits for both the service user and the mental health practitioner.

context is looked on and evaluated by external sources (e.g., sociocultural sources) and held accountable (e.g., government regulatory agencies, the legal system, third-party payment sources, and professional "watch-dogs," such as an ethics committee within a professional association). Mental health practitioners must not risk negative attributions about the quality of the services that they provide. Safeguards are derived from knowledge and use of client management and operational policies, the subject interwoven throughout this book and elaborated on in this and the next chapter particularly.

Client management refers to considering the service user to be a source of sustenance for the mental health practice. Many (most?) resources (e.g., revenues) emanate from client satisfaction AND use of efficacious interventions, regardless of type. Just as with natural resources, client management must cultivate, nurture, and protect human resources, such as the well-being and need-fulfillment objectives for service users. It is obvious, and quite acceptable, for client management to be devoted to benefits for the service user and the mental health practitioner as well.

Operational policies apply to the decisions made by the mental health practitioner that determine the factors, object and human, that impact on the professional services provided. One of the most obvious issues relevant to protection from legal challenges is recordkeeping. In this day and age, there is no justification whatsoever for allowing a practitioner to avoid or denigrate professional standards and ethics or state and federal laws relevant to clinical and business records. As with client management, operational policies provide benefits for both the service user and the mental health practitioner.

Because quality care is mandatory, the current sociocultural context encourages the mental health practitioner to maintain control of the service delivery system—as long as all systemic elements are legally and ethically appropriate. Specifically, compliance with and adherence to practitioner-determined interventions (e.g., contained in a treatment plan crafted for the benefit of the service user) must not be subject to manipulation or to being put asunder by a service user's personal characteristics, pathology, or nefarious motives. All professional interventions must be in accord with a rationale predicated on behavioral science, which will contribute significantly to quality care in the broadest sense.

THE PRACTITIONER'S PERSONAL NEEDS

Although it may seem a bit strange, the mental health practitioner's personal psychological needs play an important role in contextual and action-oriented decision making. If personal need fulfillment ends up dominating a practitioner's motivations, the logic and reason about practice-oriented decisions can be flawed and result in negative legal consequences.

A starting point for analyzing the risk created by psychological needs within the practitioner is Abraham Maslow's ideas that self-actualization is aligned with a hierarchy of need fulfillment. Hogan and Smither (2008) consider Abraham Maslow to be more influential than Sigmund Freud on personality psychology. They state that the "hierarchy of needs has become a key tool for evaluating management practices" (p. 248) and recognize that the climb up the hierarchy is not smooth as a result of blockage from real-life factors, which means that "most of us strive for goals that do not promote self-actualization" (p. 248). Consequently, if contextual considerations (e.g., the economy and income) lead the practitioner to strive to fulfill risky or inappropriate needs, the outcome can be quite negative legally.

Delving further into the contextual issues, Watson, Goldman, and Greenberg (2011) offer a gestalt model. They state:

> Gestalt therapists view life as a process of needs arising and being satisfied in a continual cycle. A dominant need emerges as figural from a background, claims attention, is satisfied, and fades into the background again. The cycle continues as new needs emerge into the foreground. Pathology or dysfunction occurs when this need-satisfaction cycle is interrupted. . . . At the action stage, need satisfaction is seen as being interrupted by introjected values. (p. 158)

In the context of mental health services, if the practitioner experiences frustration due to a declining income, lack of success in gaining referrals, or a challenge to competency (e.g., a licensing or ethics complaint), problematic ego defense mechanisms can be unleashed. McCall (1976) says "defense mechanisms may be evoked by anything that conflicts with our minimum idea of what the self must be. This might include incompetence, stupidity, selfishness, indecisiveness, or any other self-devaluating experience or circumstances" (p. 271). If this occurs, the risk of potentially negative legal consequences is obviously heightened.

My work defending mental health practitioners against complaints has revealed literally countless examples of how a practitioner has done something that is "totally out of character." Upon gaining familiarity with the situation, it emerges that the practitioner was experiencing a lack of need fulfillment, such as in the profession (e.g., criticism by colleagues, inadequate income for preferred life style, etc.) or domestic life (e.g., dissonance with a spouse or partner, debts, health problems within the family, etc.), and there was an illogical reliance on fulfilling needs that are unacceptable to professionalism, thereby triggering the complaints. For example, there have been a great number of practitioners with complaints filed against them who, after having lived lifetimes of impeccable honesty, fall on "hard-scrabble" times and resort to fraudulent practices (e.g., billing insurance companies for services that were not provided) or their conservative life styles are replaced by foolhardy actions (e.g., drug abuse, indiscriminate sexual relations, or crimes).

What is the mental health practitioner's solution to this dilemma? It is much the same as would be prescribed for a client: self-understanding to improve the quality and acceptability of decisions and actions for personal need fulfillment. As Watson et al. (2011) assert, there should be a focus on "what is occurring at the contact boundaries between self and others," and work to enhance "awareness of their own processes, needs, and wants. . . . Awareness is seen as leading to choice, thus allowing the person to choose how to behave" (p. 159).

Given their professional training, it is somewhat surprising how many practitioners respond to risks, criticisms, or challenges to their judgments or actions with the same defense mechanisms relied on by everyday folks. For example, it is not uncommon for a mental health practitioner to rationalize (i.e., explain away by illogical or irrational clarifications), project (i.e., attribute one's own motives, thoughts, or weaknesses to an external source or someone else), and displace (camouflage the goal of a motive). Although this propensity is manifested in an array of contextual considerations, it is, of course, particularly apparent in failing to maintain an appropriate plan (e.g., inadequate recordkeeping), entering into inappropriate multiple relationships (e.g., sexual or business misconduct with a service user), and engaging in fraud (e.g., after-the-fact falsification of documents, blatant lying).

Perhaps parenthetically, in being trained to be a mental health professional, a common mantra for a practitioner is "Convey unconditional positive regard to clients, because it will help the 'goodness of the person' emerge." To the contrary, in being trained as a lawyer, a common law school mantra is "Trust no one; every client lies or only gives a partial or misleading account of the facts." A second law school mantra is "No one tells another person all of the information, only what he or she wants the other person to believe" (this same idea has, of course, long been in psychological assessment textbooks, relevant to self-report instruments). With great regret, I must give the law school mantras constant consideration when I am defending mental health practitioners against legal actions.

MISLEADING REPORTS FROM OTHER MENTAL HEALTH PRACTITIONERS

Long ago, A. J. Edwards (1964), distinguished by his research on psychological assessment, said pithily that a client's responses, even to an objective test (e.g., the hallowed Minnesota Multiphasic Personality Inventory), should be viewed as only revealing what the client believes is acceptable and is willing to, consciously or unconsciously, acknowledge to another person; that is, statements about the self should not be considered to always be a realistic portrayal of the facts. In modern practice, this viewpoint is widely accepted and considered to be the social desirability response set: "the tendency for examinees to answer in what they believe are socially desirable directions, rather than answering in a way that is truly characteristic" (Van Ornum et al., 2008, p. 522).

A classic example of misleading information is found in the surveys of incomes conducted by professional associations (and other sources). From personal knowledge, it is known that, in true social desirability response set fashion, the reports about incomes are (almost?) always much higher than the reality.

As a specific example, one would think that a psychologist with a doctorate from a major APA-accredited school, two decades of impressive experience, and named a Diplomate by the American Board of Professional Psychology (ABPP) would be making a big income. In modern times, such is not necessarily the situation.

Due to the contemporary societal conditions, high fees for mental health services are in peril. Consider that fact that in the United States (and many other countries) there is a population subjected to high unemployment, fees controlled by managed care companies, and an abundance of licensed mental health professionals—which also result in much less priority for mental health services in the lives of everyday folks.

Combining the hierarchy of needs model with the tendency for social desirability responses, there is legal safety in not relying on the information or advice provided by other mental health practitioners. Of course, if the information achieves reliable status for being "evidence based," it can and should be considered, but consensus on a survey among practitioners does not necessarily establish reliability.

The ease of dispensing opinions on a listserv is especially hazardous. It is not unusual for a practitioner to post a thumbnail sketch of a case, believing that because no names are mentioned, there is no violation of confidentiality and the opinions elicited from other members of the listserv will justify an appropriate action. Both of those assumptions can be wrong.

> *The ease of dispensing opinions on a listserv is especially hazardous. It is not unusual for a practitioner to post a thumbnail sketch of a case, believing that because no names are mentioned, there is no violation of confidentiality and the opinions elicited from other members of the listserv will justify an appropriate action. Both of those assumptions can be wrong.*

The demarcation point for unprofessional conduct is defined, to a large extent, by the statutes, cases, and administrative code rules of the jurisdiction in which the professional services were provided. In conducting a deposition of a mental health practitioner, it would be potentially appropriate for the deposing attorney to ask whether there had been any posts about the case, request copies of the posts, and demand contact information for respondents to the practitioner's posts (how these issues would play out in the long run depends on the particular jurisdiction).

Moreover, a non-attorney who dispenses "legal advice" on a particular case may be held accountable for the unauthorized practice of law. It is a common misconception for a mental health professional to believe that "in my complaint case, I learned that the law requires . . ." and to assume that personal experience can be generalized to another practitioner's complaint case. One of the first things taught in law school is that an attorney should be able to distinguish any and every legal case from previous cases.

In one situation, a mental health practitioner admitted, to an attorney, to having never heard of "illegal fee-splitting," and had been operating by what three other mental health practitioners had allegedly advised. If so, the practitioner had been steered into potential insurance fraud.

Also recall the earlier comments about need fulfillment. When Practitioner 1 is told by Practitioner 2 that Practitioner 2's fee is X dollars per hour, Practitioner 1 should take it with the proverbial "grain of salt." Many instances have revealed that the professed hourly fee is elevated from the actual fee billed. This seems particularly relevant to forensic psychologists and neuropsychologists, and to psychologists who are minions for managed care companies.

For example, a common scenario is for a forensic psychologist or neuropsychologist (and some practitioners in other disciplines and specialties) to "discount" the hourly fee considerably in order to get a referral. Moreover, if a practitioner, after having provided clinical interventions, attempts to elevate a fee for services connected to the legal system, there is a distinct possibility that the court could deem it to be "gouging." That is, the clinical client needs the particular clinical practitioner's testimony to assist the judge or jury. Judges have been known to order a token fee (e.g., $10 per hour) for such "gouging" transgressions by a mental health practitioner.

Some of these legally oriented situations, regardless of the mental health specialty or discipline, involve the practitioner providing services under a so-called letter of protection. A "letter of protection" (infrequently referred to as a letter of guarantee) states that the forensic psychologist (or other type of mental health practitioner) will receive neither retainer nor payments until the case is concluded ("all payments will be delayed until a judgment is obtained"), and then the psychological (or mental health) services will be paid from the proceeds collected (Woody, 2011b, p. 362).

For example, a forensic psychologist might tell another practitioner about the high fee commanded for testimony in a court case, but not mention that the services are being provided at the risk of a letter of protection that could lead to a discounted or no payment.

A most troubling scenario often occurs with the exchange of incomes between practitioners. Many times, Practitioner 1 will report feeling like a failure because Practitioner 2 reported a very high income (much like the higher per hour issue described earlier). Having been privy to the income tax returns of Practitioner 2, I have been aware (but because of attorney-client cannot say) that the reported high figure is fiction. This sort of false information can obviously feed into the self-disillusionment within the need fulfillment model.

COMMUNITY STANDARDS

Relying on what is reported to be the "community standard" (i.e., what other similar practitioners in the community are doing) creates another contextual vulnerability. This is much like relying on what a practitioner in another jurisdiction claims is correct legally for a mental health practice, while ignoring that the issue at hand is determined by the laws pertaining to a different jurisdiction. There may be relevance to some degree, but the information will not necessarily be determinative.

Historically, but much less so today, community standards for practice were considered and often weighted heavily by courts and other tribunals (including local and state ethics committees) (Keeton, Dobbs, Keeton, & Owen, 1984). The original justification was that communication of research that occurred in New York was unlikely to reach a rural practitioner in a small town on the American prairie. Obviously the surge of electronic media and proliferation of continuing education opportunities have clearly negated that justification.

CONCLUSION

At the beginning of this chapter, comments were made about interpersonal relationships with the emphasis on the characteristics (e.g., psychological needs) of the practitioner. Throughout this book, the relations between the practitioner and clients are explored. Often information obtained from nonauthoritative sources is unreliable, which can prove to be misleading. More will be said later (see chapters Six and Seven) about obtaining authoritative information as being a required component of the "cost of doing business," such as paying for professional advice and services from accountants and attorneys.

At this point, it is appropriate to recognize the importance of others who gain admission to the practitioner's inner-sanctum for practice: staff and colleagues. Chapter Six, which is on structuring and operating a mental health business, will consider the human resources—partners, associates, and support staff—that constitute an important part of the practice context.

SIX

Business Savvy: Structuring and Operating a Mental Health Business

One of the most common complaints heard from mental health practitioners in independent practice is that they lack knowledge of how to handle the business aspects. They are comfortable with their clinical skills and are highly motivated to succeed, but they keep encountering stumbling blocks caused by not understanding the nature of the business world.

In a nutshell, the problem stems, not from personal limitations but from the indoctrination and neglect in professional training. Because mental health services are framed in "professionalism," most training programs, appropriately, give great emphasis to benevolence and fulfilling the requisite contribution to the betterment of society.

When a proposal for a graduate course on the business aspects of mental health practice was submitted to one faculty review committee, angry allegations erupted, denouncing the professor and asserting that there should be no course containing any business-related information in mental health training programs. Also, one state licensing board refused to approve any business-related seminar for continuing education credit, as did a national professional association.

Although honorable in intent (as far as it goes), the social service orientation results in neglect of certain topics, types of information, and skills that are essential to effective mental health practice, namely formulating, developing, and maintaining business savvy in the provision of professional services. Consequently, many mental health practitioners end up not achieving their full potential for bettering society, and everyone loses.

The old saying "What price valor?" comes to mind. Maximizing the likelihood of internalization of professionalism by the student or trainee and ignoring and minimizing the recognition of essential modern business ideas, abilities, laws, and ethics leads to fewer benefits for society, service users, and practitioners.

Mental health practitioners lacking authoritative knowledge and ability for identifying and analyzing business conditions and factors cannot move to developing an adequate service delivery plan.

Mental health practitioners lacking authoritative knowledge and ability for identifying and analyzing business conditions and factors cannot move to developing an adequate service delivery plan. Not only are the service users potentially deprived of quality, the practitioners attempting to operate without business-related acumen will be in a free-fall without an all-important safety net for avoiding legal and ethical problems. Moreover, the latter places revenues in grave jeopardy, and without reasonable financial compensation, practice success is not apt to occur.

This chapter focuses on two primary settings: (1) agency and (2) independent practice. The comments distinguishing these two options are intended to allow idiosyncratic considerations and adaptations by the given mental health professional.

AGENCY PRACTICE

Agency practice refers to being affiliated, either as an employee or independent contractor (these terms will be defined later) with a group practice, commonly chartered with the state government as a "non-profit" or "charitable" organization. It should be recognized that being "non-profit" is a misnomer.

Non-profit agencies may have various payment arrangements, including some services that are *pro bono publico*, which is Latin for "for the public good," provided to selected people without charge. It is common for a true non-profit agency to support social causes, such as providing help to persons who have suffered abuse, the homeless, religious organizations, and so on. However, there also are non-profit agencies that are quasi-commercial, that is, are pursuing revenues or fees to pay those who are in the administration or service channels of the organizations. This is not illogical, because any service organization has to have funding to "keep the doors open."

Regrettably, occasionally there are sham charitable organizations, in which the members of the board of directors (as required by the government for the agency to enjoy certain tax benefits) are selected to accommodate camouflaged benefits for the founders, administrators, and others more than for needy beneficiaries. Yes, this could be criminal conduct, and an efficient government would monitor for this sort of potential fraud closely, but regrettably these nefarious entities often go unattended.

On the matter of professionalism, there have been many instances in which a charitable organization is exempt from some legal requirements that would be imposed on an independent practice. Sometimes the exemptions are done surreptitiously but sometimes they have authorization from state statutes. That is, due to donations to and effective lobbying of the political sources (e.g., members of a state legislature), a non-profit social cause can get a statute passed and ratified that will allow certain agencies to bypass professionally endorsed standards (e.g., mandatory use of licensed practitioners). These legal exemptions vary among jurisdictions.

One agency director, ostensibly with the endorsement of the board of directors (but with no state statutory justification), required all of the family therapists to make no record entries that might have negative effects in a court case of any kind, even if the information was relevant and material to the clinical aspects of the services. Of course any individual therapist employed in the agency could still be subject to potential discipline from a state licensing board that had a statutory mandate or an administrative code rule for recordkeeping by licensed mental health practitioners. Moreover, from a public policy point of view, the agency director was clearly making legal requirements inconsequential, and contradicting proper commitment to supporting the legal system.

For the individual mental health practitioner, the message is simple: There should be no affiliation with any agency, no matter how seemingly well established, without adequate investigation of its legality

For the individual mental health practitioner, the message is simple: There should be no affiliation with any agency, no matter how seemingly well established, without adequate investigation of its legality and professionalism.

and professionalism. Just because a charitable agency chooses not to adhere to the law, standards, or ethics, it does not mean the licensed mental health practitioner may choose to ignore legal and ethical standards.

What if the agency imposes some non-professional requirement on a licensed mental health practitioner? It is common for ethics codes to require the practitioner to try to remedy the conflict. On a more legal level, a practitioner who commits a violation as a result of instruction from an employer can still be held accountable. If a situation arises in which the practitioner is pressed into non-professional conduct and the situation cannot be corrected, there is little choice but to terminate the affiliation with the agency immediately; there also may be a need to be a "whistle blower" concerning the wrongful conduct. Seeking qualified legal counsel for troubling situations such as this ilk is advised, rather than asking the advice of another mental health practitioner.

INDEPENDENT PRACTICE

The term "independence" is pivotal for a definition of independent mental health practice. VandenBos (2007) defines "independence" as "freedom from the influence or control of other individuals or groups" (p. 474). It seems self-evident ("perceived immediately by the mind to be true without need of supporting argument or empirical evidence," p. 830) that no active mental health practitioner—even if in full-time solo (no close colleagues) private practice (self-employment)—is truly free from the influence or control of others.

Perhaps the cornerstone for a definition of independent mental health practice is being self-determining about the professional services that are being provided, not the source of revenues per se: "control of one's behavior by internal convictions and decisions rather than by external demands" (p. 829). If this concept is accepted, a mental health practitioner could, for example, choose to work for an agency, teach a university course as an adjunct professor, provide clinical services to clients, write for scholarly publication, and consult periodically with organizations and still be an "independent practitioner." To attempt to discount the self-determination factor by pointing to revenues coming on a regular basis from teaching a course at the university would be faulty; revenues coming on a regular basis from clinical clients are much the same in nature.

STRUCTURING A MENTAL HEALTH PRACTICE

Some mental health practitioners have the misguided notion that going into independent practice depends primarily on being licensed and having clinical skills, as would be achieved by knowledge, training, supervision, and experience. Of course being qualified academically is a prerequisite for practice, but it is not enough.

Similarly, a goodly number of mental health professionals believe that establishing a practice is simply finding an office to rent, getting letterhead stationery and business cards, and getting one's availability and qualifications into the minds of potential service users and referral sources. Again, although necessary at some point, those things are not enough for an inauguration into practice.

Following up on the ideas presented in Chapter Five about the practice context, there are prerequisites to deciding on the structure of a mental health practice. A myriad of contextual factors that potentially will impact on the operations must be considered. Among the literally countless considerations are: accepting a business orientation that will accommodate both professionalism and commercialism; embracing entrepreneurship; determining how to penetrate the existing mental health marketplace; and obtaining adequate resources (human resources, personal qualities, professional knowledge and skills, and financial support) to establish and maintain the effectiveness and qualities necessary for legally safe and professionally acceptable service delivery.

THE BUSINESS MINDSET

The guidance for clinical and other professional services provided throughout this book becomes reality within a business framework.

Because of the "Ivory Tower" framework and academic considerations, university and professional training programs tend to minimize, perhaps even ignore, the need to inculcate an informed and effective business model for the provision of mental health services. Without astute business awareness, the mental practitioner is vulnerable to decreased quality care and elevated risk of failure.

In providing mental health services, the business mindset should be founded on compatibility with professionalism. As mentioned at the beginning of this chapter, professional training programs, appropriately, give great emphasis to benevolence and fulfilling the requisite contribution to better-ment of society. Walfish and Barnett (2009) state that the first principle for being a private practitioner is "You need to resolve the conflict between altruism and being a business owner" (p. 8), and they add, "If you are helpful to most people, you need not feel guilty for making money and being successful" (p. 9).

Entrepreneurship

The business mindset should accept that entrepreneurship is mandatory for success. An entrepreneur must be a good communicator, salesperson, manager of time and resources, analyst of influences, creator of ideas and plans, and leader of others. J. E. Baron and Shane (2008) describe entrepreneurship as a complex process that must be ongoing. They believe that opportunities must be conceived and recognized, resources must be located and used wisely, uncertainty must be tolerated, and the entrepreneur must have self-confidence, high energy, passion for success and goal attainment, and operating and marketing vision. The latter qualities are, of course, compatible with what research identifies as necessary for effective leadership (Bryman, 1992; Norhouse, 2009).

Targeting and Reaching a Viable Market Sector

When beginning a mental health practice, a threshold challenge is to identify a market. Yes, the word "market" is apt. As said throughout this book, the words "client" and "patient" generally have been replaced with "service user" and "consumer."

At one time, certain laws and professional ethics imposed restraints on marketing health care services. For example, some ethics codes once prescribed and proscribed advertising details, such as no use of bold print or box advertisements. Bloom (1976) provides a description of the negative stance that existed in the past: "Advertising has been accused of being misleading, expensive, wasteful, anticompetitive, inflationary, offensive, intrusive, and even immoral" (p. 1). But there was a counter viewpoint: "In theory, advertising that distributes information can help consumers make better economic decisions" (McDaniel, Smith, & Smith, 1986, p. 134).

Ethical and legal restrictions ran counter to the preferences of the Federal Trade Commission (FTC, 1979). After a series of legal cases—relevant to the First Amendment—the FTC ruled that advertising restrictions "served to deprive consumers of the free flow of information about the availability of health care services, to deter the offering of innovative forms of health care and to stifle the rise of almost every type of health care delivery that could potentially pose a threat to the income of the fee-for-service physicians in private practice. The costs to the public in terms of less expensive or even, perhaps, more improved forms of medical service are great" (p. 917).

Soon after this ruling, legislatures implemented changes in the laws relevant to advertising pertaining to health care (Walker, 1979). The major mental health professional associations also altered their ethics codes accordingly.

Today it is quite appropriate and, indeed, necessary for survival to use essentially any affordable marketing modality. The primary legal guideline is that any promotional communication must be honest and not misleading. Professional ethics follow that idea, but may set forth definite actions. For example, psychologists are expected to avoid false or deceptive statements, not solicit testimonials from vulnerable persons (e.g., current clients), and limit in-person solicitations (American Psychological Association, 2002).

> *Today it is quite appropriate and, indeed, necessary for survival to use essentially any affordable marketing modality. The primary legal guideline is that any promotional communication must be honest and not misleading.*

In terms of targeting a market sector, just because another practitioner in the community offers a particular type of service does not mean that the marketplace cannot support another practitioner of the same type. When there is competition for the same clientele, success will depend on marketing, perhaps even more than on clinical skills or longevity per se.

Some mental health practitioners have the notion that aggressive advertising of many types of services is wise. In fact, there is reason to believe that limiting professional services to tried and true competencies is best. One cannot be a master of every type of service. Usually by sticking to established competencies, the practitioner becomes recognized in the marketplace as the best source for a given type of service, and the likelihood is that the practice will be strengthened, including financially.

Adequate Resources

Start-up expenses can prove to be more than expected. Foolish practitioners borrow large sums of money to tailor offices to a seeming level of success that is neither achievable nor realistic. For example, some mental health practitioners enter into a long-term lease in a "high-rent" building, only to find that the space is unaffordable (a financial recession certainly raises the specter of changes in affordability). Appearances do not determine success.

Human resources are highly important, possibly more so than the location of the practice. The mental health practitioner is potentially vicariously liable for anyone associated with the practice. Thus, for example, if a secretary breaches patient confidentiality or commits insurance fraud (due to either incompetence or criminal intent), the mental health practitioner may well be held accountable for alleged negligent supervision by a licensing board, third-party payment source, or the legal system. Said simply: A mental health practitioner is known by the company that he or she keeps. If there is a shared enterprise, the "innocent" practitioner may have legal (vicarious or imputed) liability.

Another arrangement that merits consideration is being associated with another mental health practitioner and whether the associate should work as an independent contractor or an employee. In addition to potential vicarious liability from any sort of professional relationship, an independent contractor arrangement must be truly independent; this means that a senior practitioner who accepts an associate into the mental health practice must avoid controls, such as having a noncompetition agreement.

The Internal Revenue Service sets forth criteria that distinguish independent contractors from employees, and violation of these criteria can lead to severe penalties—bluntly stated, the government, at all levels, wants appropriate employment-related taxes to be paid. Obviously, determining whether a professional relationship does or does not accommodate an independent contractor arrangement requires authoritative knowledge of laws and taxation, and points definitely to the need for advice from attorneys and accountants.

Noncompetition Agreements

It is understandable that a senior practitioner, after years of effort and money, would not want an associate, whether an independent contractor or an employee, to "steal the clientele." State laws typically specify what is "unfair competition," as justifies noncompetition and nonsolicitation contracts. What is specified in one (state) jurisdiction may or may not be the same in another jurisdiction. Further, this is a topic in which ethics may clash with what is legal.

For example, in a state with laws that clearly legitimized noncompetition and nonsolicitation contracts, Practitioner 1 invested years of effort and considerable money in developing a successful clinic. Practitioner 1 employed Practitioner 2 for several years. The employment had been prefaced by a written agreement that Practitioner 2 would not set up a private practice within X-number of miles or solicit the clientele that Practitioner 2 had seen during the employment. The terms and conditions were in accord with the laws of the particular jurisdiction.

Practitioner 1 (employer) discovered that Practitioner 2 (employee) had set up a practice nearby (closer than what was agreed to in the employment contract) and had told the Practitioner 1 that certain clients had ended treatment. In point of fact, Practitioner 2 had been surreptitiously transferring these clients over to his new independent practice.

The written agreement between Practitioner 1 and Practitioner 2 specified that, upon termination of employment, the employer and employee would meet together with the clients being served by the departing employee and encourage (but not require) them to be seen by other qualified associates in the employer's clinic. Because of Practitioner 2's indiscretions (i.e., alleged breach of contract), Practitioner 1 terminated Practitioner 2.

Each filed regulatory complaints against the other, highlighting the noncompetition aspects of the employment contract. The licensing agency dismissed both complaints, basically because client welfare had not been jeopardized and the particular state's laws supported the contract. As a follow up, Practitioner 1 filed a lawsuit for a restraining order requiring Practitioner 2 to honor the contract, and the court ruled in favor of Practitioner 1.

Not to be outdone, Practitioner 2 enlisted a former client to file an ethics complaint with a professional association, alleging that the employer should not have had contractual terms that would allow Practitioner 1, under any circumstances, to be in the confidential treatment room with the clients previously served by Practitioner 2 (even though the clients were clearly embraced by the business framework owned by Practitioner 1). With complete disregard for the legal decisions made by the regulatory agency and the court of law, the professional association reprimanded Practitioner 1.

The foregoing example is one reason why some mental health practitioners believe that the contemporary business framework imposed legally leads them to drop membership in professional associations. Indeed, there does, in fact, seem to be greater compatibility between modern business conditions and the law, with estrangement from some of the restraints in ethics codes imposed by certain professional associations.

As I have stated previously, my personal opinion is that often there is far less bias, prejudice, and discrimination in the decisions made by a court than in licensing board and ethics committee proceedings.

Time Management

Time is a resource, and must be managed well. Because income usually is dependent on billable hours, independent mental health practitioners are prone to believe there should be no restriction on the time spent practicing—if there is a potential client wanting an appointment, the quest for revenue justifies setting aside other considerations, such as family life and health risks. This is foolish.

Recall the old adage: "too busy for your own good." Basically, every practitioner must give strong preference to operations that are efficient (adequate for the task) and timely (accomplished promptly). Depending on assistants, such as a secretary, is certainly fine for some things, but there must always be meaningful supervision of staff and clinical associates by the mental health practitioner (remember vicarious liability). Poor management due to lack of supervision is inexcusable and creates a distinct risk of regulatory and ethics complaints. A well-defined manual should set forth detailed policies for everyone in the practice to follow. Oversight for adherence to the policies must not be neglected.

Finally, being overly busy or not getting things done in an efficient or timely manner can be a harbinger of ill health for the mental health practitioner. One of the foremost resources of any practice is a fully functioning practitioner. Depleted physical or mental strength can only lead to increased risk of failure.

CONCLUSION

Whether the practice is with an agency or independent, and regardless of professional discipline, modern mental health practitioners are required to demonstrate strict adherence to the laws of the particular state. In some instances, there may be a conflict between relevant laws and professional ethics. Given the potential for punishment, it seems to be a "no brainer"— law should trump ethics. However, if the practitioner is uncomfortable with a law versus ethics conflict, professionalism supports that the practitioner, rather than violating either, should try to reconcile the differences, such as by making adaptations in services that would accommodate both sources.

Although often neglected in university and professional training programs, the mental health practitioner must establish and maintain business policies and operations that are consonant with accepting a business orientation that will accommodate both professionalism and commercialism; embracing entrepreneurship; knowing how to penetrate the existing mental health marketplace; and having adequate human resources, personal qualities, professional knowledge and skills, and financial support. Doing so will help practitioners attain effectiveness and the qualities necessary for legally safe and professionally acceptable service delivery, with quality care and risk management for the benefit of society, service users, and themselves.

SEVEN

Dealing With Attorneys and the Legal System

In order to develop legal safeguards for mental health practices, the threshold issue for the practitioner is to understand the legal system, be able to work within the context, and work with the participants. Mental health practitioners usually are not prepared for involvement in an adversarial context. Consequently, attorneys (trained to thrive on assertive conduct and well-honed persuasion skills) are likely to be unresponsive to efforts by mental health practitioners to resolve conflicts by verbal exchanges alone—there must be adherence to the legal rules as set forth in the particular jurisdiction.

In today's litigious world, all mental health practitioners need to be knowledgeable about how to respond to discovery tactics, such as depositions, subpoenas, and court orders. If uninformed, the practitioner risks a potentially negative encounter with a well-prepared adversary, the outcome of which can be quite detrimental to the practitioner, such as

In today's litigious world, all mental health practitioners need to be knowledgeable about how to respond to discovery tactics, such as depositions, subpoenas, and court orders. If uninformed, the practitioner risks a potentially negative encounter with a well-prepared adversary, the outcome of which can be quite detrimental to the practitioner, such as loss of current and future income, a licensing and/or ethics complaint, and possibly a lawsuit.

loss of current and future income, a licensing and/or ethics complaint, and possibly a lawsuit.

In this chapter, practical suggestions will be made to identify the considerations that are unique to the practitioner's jurisdiction, with strong emphasis on obtaining legal counsel from within the jurisdiction (as opposed to relying on a national "hotline" that is proffered as an inducement to purchasing a given malpractice policy or becoming a member of a professional association), albeit legal counsel is an additional, but essential, "cost of doing business." Information also will be given on how to prepare records (from the outset of services) that will be optimally appropriate for legal matters and how to communicate in depositions and courtroom testimony.

THE RULE OF LAW

It is an understatement to say that law is omnipresent in modern life. From the point of view of social relationships, whether commercial or personal, there are legal principles to which a person must adhere. As Feinman (2010) puts it:

> Today the law affects us individually when we rent apartments [or office suites for mental health practice] or own homes, marry, drive cars, borrow money, purchase goods, belong to organizations, go to school or work, and obtain health care, and collectively when the government taxes, regulates the airways and cyberspace, polices crimes and controls pollution. (pp. 2–3)

Law certainly controls the contemporary mental health professions, much more so now than in the past; the future portends to introduce even greater legal controls over everyday life. Foremost for mental health practitioners, there are legal determinants of who can provide mental health services, the necessary quality care (practices to implement and avoid), and financial opportunities (reimbursement policies and resources, such as through Medicare).

Indeed, there has been a steady diminution of "personal preference" in mental health services, which reaches into the so-called therapeutic alliance. Neither the practitioner nor the service user is allowed by society to define the professional relationship in a manner that is incompatible with the framework containing values, ethics, and beliefs endorsed by society and, consequently, the law.

Given that this book is devoted, in part, to risk management, the topic of dealing with attorneys should be viewed from three perspectives. First, the mental health practitioner needs to understand the "professional culture" in which an attorney operates—for the moment, suffice it to say that it is far different from the cultural considerations for a mental health practitioner. Second, the mental health practitioner must be able to avoid creating risks with attorneys—in this high-risk era, one of the last things that a sensible and prudent mental practitioner would want is to have an attorney as an "enemy." Third, for risk management (which benefits both the practitioner and the service user), the mental health practitioner must develop allies—these may include accountants, consultants on special issues, and—foremost—an attorney for legal counsel.

THE PROFESSIONAL CULTURE FOR ATTORNEYS

There are considerable differences between the cultures of the mental health clinic and the courtroom. Each venue has it unique context, in which idiosyncratic cultural factors exist.

In the mental health clinic (or office), the culture is defined by professional services that remediate or cure. The desired outcome in the legal culture also is problem solving; however, legal "interventions" and "problem-solving" bear little connection to those of mental health services. In the mental health context, the end objective is healing, and the participants are co-facilitators. However, in the legal context, the participants are ostensibly adversaries.

In a defining treatise for forensic mental health services, Slovenko (1973) referred to the adversary method as "gamesmanship under the gavel" and a "sporting theory of justice" (p. 4), derived from the drama in the circumstances. He points out that, "The court does not entertain moot controversies," whereas, "The work of science, on the other hand, is a corporate effort which attempts to ascertain empirical relationships through the examination of repeated instances and has for its purpose the growth of a body of general principles" (p. 8). Assuming that the mental health practitioner accepts the scientist-practitioner model, there is allegiance to measurement (e.g., mathematics or statistics) and truth is determined by loyalty to the service user.

The legal effort is to establish truth, with an explanation, as determined by the trier-of-fact (the judge and the jury) according to certain rules and laws promulgated by the government and society. Although not perfect for objectivity, the legal process fulfills the tenets of justice that have been defined, accepted, and enforced by society. In mental health services, truth is subjectively determined within the professional relationship, and may or may not be acted on, depending on laws and professional ethics and standards.

There is one more shared commonality. Neither mental health services or legal services have sure-fire outcomes because life is complex and unpredictable (that statement alone could be the topic of a voluminous book!). Both mental health and legal problems defy simple solutions.

In view of the foregoing differences, it is not surprising that, "When psychologists become involved with the legal system, they may, initially at least, feel like a 'stranger in a strange land'" (Shapiro & Smith, 2011, p. 149), along with a sense of vulnerability. The culture for attorneys fosters forceful and purposeful communication; the mental health culture expects facilitative communication. Said only partially facetiously in law school, the would-be attorney has a Super Hero mentality cultivated and a strong backbone implanted; in graduate mental health training programs, the would-be mental health practitioner is taught to show deference to people with mental disorders and has (figuratively) his or her backbone removed. Stated bluntly, the culture of attorneys embraces strength and assertiveness, two characteristics that receive little or no attention in the mental health practitioners' culture.

In defense of the culture for attorneys, it should be underscored that, according to the esteemed jurist, Benjamin N. Cardozo (1921), "The final cause of law is the welfare of society" (p. 66). Incidentally, Cardozo's acceptance that the legal system is not perfect (e.g., judges' have idiosyncrasies) is reminiscent of the justification for the imperfections in mental health services professed by the iconic Frederick C. Thorne (1961), who said: "Even in view of the admitted invalidity or relative inefficiency of many clinical decisions, society must depend upon clinical decisions because of the practical and economic limitations of life situations" (p. 23).

AVOIDING ALIENATION OF ATTORNEYS

Because there are different cultural factors present in the legal system and in mental health services, it is not surprising the two professional frameworks, at times, may become confrontational (in a reasonably courteous but less than friendly way). Some mental health practitioners try to ignore the legal system. For example, a mental health practitioner told me pathetically about being "picked up by deputies, placed in a cell in a orange jumpsuit, and taken in chains to face a judge for ignoring a subpoena." The definition of professionalism imposes an axiom on mental health practitioners to support and honor the legal system.

Perhaps part of a mental health practitioner's denial of support for the legal system comes from the fact that mental health programs seldom provide adequate training relevant to understanding and participating in the legal process. As will be discussed in the next section, safeguards come from having competent allies, particularly an attorney for legal counsel.

Some mental health practitioners harbor negative opinions of attorneys. Given their different cultures and knowledge composites, this negativity is not surprising. In keeping with principles of social and evolutionary psychology, it is known that those who are different from ourselves (e.g., from a different culture, race, or tribe) are viewed with suspicion and defensiveness.

The cornerstone for suspicion may be that attorneys are duty bound to be zealous advocates of their clients' legal interests, which includes persuading others, such as mental health practitioners, to favor their clients. It is not surprising that there is dissonance between the attorney and the mental health professional.

An attorney's knowledge and use of legal procedures and rules (commonly unknown to and unappreciated by mental health practitioners), such as use of a subpoena or court order to obtain confidential records, may strike some mental health professionals as an unwarranted attempt to wrest control and autonomy away from the mental health service provider. From the legal perspective, these forceful strategies are in accord

From the legal perspective, these forceful strategies are in accord with the legal duties imposed on an attorney, namely using the law to manifest client advocacy.

with the legal duties imposed on an attorney, namely using the law to manifest client advocacy.

When this clash of the titans occurs, the mental health practitioner can, and often should, acquire legal counsel. Because mental health practitioners are not commonly well trained for adversarial scenarios and typically want to avoid even essential expenses (due to their lack of preparation for the business aspects of mental health services), any dispute involving legal procedures and rules ends up being a David versus Goliath situation. Attorney versus attorney on a matter pertaining to mental health services is the surest way to ensure the rights of the mental health practitioner. Investing in legal counsel is unquestionably a necessary expense.

When confronted with a legal situation, the mental health practitioner should maintain two conditions: (1) demonstrate full and proper cooperation with the legal system and the attorneys; and (2) avoid inappropriate views or conduct. These two conditions require legal knowledge and orientation that often (usually) must be derived from the practitioner's own legal counsel—a legal ally.

At all times, the mental health practitioner should avoid incurring the wrath of an attorney. The following are seven ways that will almost certainly whet the appetite of any attorney to "teach a lesson about legal procedure" to a mental health practitioner, and to do so with a less than pleasant tone. Here are seven actions that should be avoided by a mental health practitioner:

1. Try to control the attorney. Even though a practitioner has a high-level of specialized training in a mental health discipline, the legal arena is not the "home court" and trying to "outsmart" an attorney is a surefire way to lose the match.
2. Ignore the legal process, such as not responding properly to a subpoena or court order.
3. Fail to deal with fees from the outset and fail to respond to a written contractual agreement with the service user.
4. Inflate the fee for forensic services above the regular clinical fee.
5. Charge excessively for preparation time, such as reviewing clinical records.
6. Keep records, information, or opinions from the attorney, especially if there has been a valid subpoena or court order.
7. Act emotionally.

The reality is that contemporary mental health services are subject to legal prescriptions and proscriptions to which many mental health practitioners cannot respond adequately without allies.

HAVING ALLIES

When encountering a practice situation with legal issues, the mental health practitioner might be tempted to talk to another mental health practitioner, attend a seminar taught by a forensic psychologist, try to find a quick answer from google.com, or read a book. One problem with these solutions is that the mental health or forensic (non-attorney) practitioner, although well intended, usually has only a partial understanding of the law overall (often based on his or her personal experiences rather than on any formal law school education). Another problem is that misinformation can be disseminated in seminars, articles, or collegial discussions or the information can be misinterpreted by the mental health practitioner.

The non-attorney may believe that because a given legal principle was present in a past case, it should be applicable now. Even if the principle were relevant and material to the situation at hand, judges have been known to not follow precedent (Spohn & Hemmens, 2009). Moreover, once in the courtroom, every attorney is armed with techniques for distinguishing one case from another.

There also is a risk of partial or misinformation from consulting with an attorney who is not familiar with and admitted to the state bar in the jurisdiction(s) in which the mental health services occur. Numerous examples of incorrect legal counsel have been noted in information on the World Wide Web and from free legal consultation offered by an attorney affiliated with a professional organization or insurance company located elsewhere. Said simply, laws differ among jurisdictions.

Therefore, there are two irrefutable axioms. First, the legal system must be accommodated. Anyone who declares, "I won't appear in court" is, to say the least, ignorant of the law and at extreme risk of incurring negative legal consequences. Second, there is an old adage that applies to attorneys and mental health practitioners alike: "A person who represents himself in legal matters has a fool for a client." Certainly relying on someone other than a qualified attorney is foolhardy.

Moreover, it is prudent to have allies with varied types of expertise. Given the need to have clear and impeccable financial records, especially relevant to third-party payment sources and taxation, a well-trained accountant should be available to the mental health practitioner. As is true of mental health practitioners, accountants and attorneys do not have expertise in all aspects of their chosen profession, and usually have little or no knowledge about a mental health practice. It is important to determine whether or not an ally, notwithstanding seemingly impeccable credentials, is competent for the issues of concern to the mental health practitioner. Warning: Trying to get free accounting or legal advice in casual contacts (e.g., at a social function or when playing a sport) is foolhardy—"You get what you pay for."

CONCLUSION

People today are subject to extensive legal restrictions and mental health service practitioners are no exception. The mental health practitioner generally is ill-prepared to deal with the legal "culture." Professionals of all types who are able to participate with appropriate knowledge and skills facilitate risk management to benefit society, service users, and practitioners. For mental health practitioners, this necessitates special training, buttressed by expertise from allies, such as accountants and attorneys.

The legal and mental health professions both are committed to problem-solving; they seek truth, but they do so by the use of very different methods. The adversarial nature of the legal arena may cause the mental health practitioner to feel out of place, and because legalists are trained for "legal combat," mental health professionals should purposefully avoid alienating the legalists. Said simply, judges and attorneys are on their "home turf" and have a strong advantage in any questionable or disputed matter.

The definition of professionalism imposes an axiom on mental health practitioners to support and honor the legal system. The practitioner should maintain two conditions: (1) demonstrate full and proper cooperation with the legal system and the attorneys; and (2) avoid inappropriate views or conduct. Certainly the practitioner should maintain a mindset to avoid incurring the wrath of an attorney (recall the seven paradoxical actions that were presented in this chapter).

Misinformation abounds among mental health professionals, commonly coming from a non-attorney, such as a forensic psychologist, incorrectly believing that a personal experience in a court case generalizes to any similar legal situation. Attorneys are trained to distinguish legal cases, whereas mental health professionals are not! Legal counsel should be obtained only from an attorney who is admitted to the state bar in the jurisdiction in which the mental health practice is located. Beware of information on the World Wide Web or case-specific legal advice dispensed by attorneys for professional associations and insurance companies who are not admitted to the particular jurisdiction.

EIGHT

Threatening and Dangerous Service Users

By the 1960s, mental health services were burgeoning. Humanistic voices, such as Abraham Maslow (1970) and Carl R. Rogers (1961), were advocating a positive force within people. Perhaps this is true for those free from mental problems, but there are some people, for whatever reason(s), who resort to hostile-aggressive actions toward self or others. As support for community mental health programs decreased, practitioners were left dealing with some people who were ill suited for outpatient treatment.

Fundamentally, mental health practitioners are devoted to working with people who have cognitive, emotional, and behavioral problems. It is axiomatic that mental health service users do not make good decisions in their lives, often due to the disabilities and disorders that they suffer. Consequently, they often have engaged in unwise conduct. These are the reasons that led them to seek professional help.

Overtaxed by stress and given their patterns of early development, some service users will no doubt direct their usual ineffective interpersonal patterns toward a

Overtaxed by stress and given their patterns of early development, some service users will no doubt direct their usual ineffective interpersonal patterns toward a mental health practitioner (e.g., seeing the practitioner as threatening or untrustworthy).

mental health practitioner (e.g., seeing the practitioner as threatening or untrustworthy). When this type of desperate, futile, and illogical response emerges from a client, the practitioner must become defensive.

Being defensive toward a client is not usually a part of the training in the mental health services. To some degree, a defensive professional is the antithesis of what is advocated. The overriding objective for academic instructors is to instill a commitment in the practitioner to be benevolent, altruistic, reinforcing, deferent, empathic, and supportive relevant to service users.

Although suggestions for risk assessment and management have been offered in Chapter Four, this chapter delves further into the subject, explaining how to assess risk, as well as aggressive and threatening behavior. The risk of violence associated with mental disorders will be discussed. Specifically, the possibility of danger from service users and the triggers for violent actions will be explored. Also, recognizing the potential for violence in the context of mental health services, 10 types of potentially violent behavioral styles will be posited.

RISK AND THREAT ASSESSMENT

The modern and realistic viewpoint is that mental health practitioners must constantly assess risk and the possibility of threat from a service user, strategize efforts to circumvent an occurrence of violence, and protect themselves just as much as, if not more than, they protect the service user. Bennett et al. (2006) state: "Risk is the calculation that a particular treatment, intervention, or service will lead to a good or bad outcome and that the outcome will have positive or negative consequences" (p. 11). Bartol and Bartol (2012) offer the following definition of threat assessment: "investigative and operational activities designed to identify, assess, and manage individuals who may pose a threat of violence to *identifiable targets*," (p. 251).

Threatening communications and behaviors signal that there is danger, whether it is to self (e.g., suicide ideation) or to others (e.g., assaultive or homicidal ideation). In turn, danger is the threshold to violence, which often is directed toward those people who are closest to the perpetrator of the harm (e.g., domestic violence). Human nature supports that when a service user senses a need to blame someone else for the overwhelming pressure or problem, the mental health practitioner is apt to become a target for aggression.

Sometimes the practitioner is merely a symbol. For example, a paranoid schizophrenic former patient at Hospital A traveled a considerable distance to Hospital B, took a duffle bag with two handguns and two hundred rounds of ammunition upstairs to the chief psychiatrist's office, and shot and killed the psychiatrist. Although the psychiatrist had never treated the killer, the disordered mind concluded that it was appropriate to murder the psychiatrist because he had been employed years earlier at Hospital A where treatment (considered to be abusive by the former patient) had been received from another psychiatrist, and the psychiatrist who was targeted was easy to locate, although it took several hours of driving to get to Hospital B.

Violence is the product of aggression, which is intended to harm or injure a person, oneself, or an object (Franzoi, 2009). Hostile aggression knows no limit, and can cause injury or death to the victim. Although males tend to resort to being more physically aggressive than females (who tend to be more verbally aggressive), there appears to be a trend of both genders moving toward more inappropriate aggression and violence.

This is not the place to explore the causes of violence per se. Suffice it to say that there may be evolutionary and biological issues. For example, behavior genetics and hormonal activity may influence aggressive behavior. There is strong reason to believe that modern society reinforces aggression and violence, such as through the mass media. That is, social learning may be creating a more violent world.

[Note: At one time, there was some doubt that about the effects of watching violent depictions, such as in movies or on television, led to violence. There is no longer doubt: "Over the past 40 years, a significant amount of research literature has strongly supported the observation that media violence viewing is one factor contributing to the development of aggression and violence . . . studies have concluded that *heavy* exposure to televised violence is one of the most significant causes of violence in society" (Bartol & Bartol, 2012, p. 275). For adults, the effects from media violence may be short-term, but almost all children experience long-term effects (i.e., aggressive propensities) aligned with violence proneness from watching media violence (Huesmann, Moise-Titus, Podolski, & Eron, 2003).]

The social learning approach considers how violent behavior is acquired and maintained, and what is necessary to get violent behavior to stop. For example, the old adage "You are known by the company that you keep" should be remembered. Parents should be encouraged to minimize their child's imitative learning of aggression and violence, as would occur from observing others' aggressive or violent behaviors.

In assessing the risk of violence by the client, the mental health practitioner should consider the "social groups" with which the client has a connection, such as those that condone antisocial or violent beliefs and acts. Of course, a singular relationship could cast an adverse influence as well.

The social conditions within the community in which the vulnerable person lives can promote, accommodate, or contradict the service user's potential for violence. In the context of mental health services, risk assessment should survey group influences, how the service user deals with others, the attitudes and beliefs that are being reinforced, and indications of condoning violence.

When the service user anticipates or actually receives rewards for being violent, the risk of aggression and violence escalates. If results of reinforcement from aggression outweigh anticipated punishments, violence is more likely to occur.

Once the service user starts relying on aggression and violence, there is the possibility of a "downward spiral," that is, the service user is prone to get worse and worse, unless the mental health practitioner can achieve an effective turnaround.

Once the service user starts relying on aggression and violence, there is the possibility of a "downward spiral," that is, the service user is prone to get worse and worse, unless the mental health practitioner can achieve an effective turnaround. Helping all service users develop positive social networks is an important dimension of mental health services, regardless of the referring problem.

Relying on the research of Bandura (1979), Dutton (2003) indicates that the origins of aggression are considered as coming from: observational learning, reinforced performance, and/or structural determinants. The instigators of aggression are identified as being: modeling influences (disinhibitory, facilitative, arousing, and stimulus enhancing); aversive treatment (physical assaults, verbal threats and insults, adverse reductions in reinforcement, and thwarting); incentive inducements; instructional control; and bizarre symbolic control. The regulators of aggression include: external reinforcement (tangible rewards, social and status rewards, expression of injury, and alleviation of aversive treatment); punishment (inhibitory or informative); vicarious reinforcement (observed rewards and punishments); and self-reinforcement (self-reward, self-punishment, neutralization of self-punishment, moral justification, palliative comparison, euphemistic labeling, displacement of responsibility, diffusion of responsibility, dehumanization of victims, attribution of blame to victims, and misrepresentation of consequences).

The basic thesis is that anger is evoked to generate a sense of personal control. When anger erupts, the person demonstrates hostile-aggressive conduct. For example, when insulted, a person develops tension, and thus an urgent need to reduce or remove it. If social learning conditions provided and reinforced aggressive actions as a solution, the person will rely on aggression.

Violence seems to be the product of a chaining of factors that reflect: frustration, disappointment, aggravation, aggression, hostility, and violence. When this chaining sequence occurs in the life of a service user, the mental health practitioner can reasonably predict an increased possibility of violence toward self or others. If these factors occur in a person who has adopted a narcissistic bent and close-mindedness, the fuse for explosive behavior is burning.

If one's life becomes difficult, a mentally strong person reacts with assertiveness, achievement, and problem solving. If one's life seems to be uncontrollable, the mentally weak person reacts with blunting (e.g., substance abuse, distracting activities or thoughts) or no blunting (e.g., withdrawal or learned helplessness). Because anger releases tension, it provides both intrinsic and extrinsic rewards, albeit a false sense of self-esteem and competence through inept or illegal control of others.

A popular notion is that a person with psychological and conduct problems—or more broadly, one who receives mental health services—is more apt to be violent than the mythical "average person." There is some, but not total, truth to that assumption.

Over the years, research has revealed that:

> although most people with major mental disorder do not engage in violence, the likelihood of committing violence is greater for people with a major mental disorder than for those without; substance misuse raises the risk of violence by people with mental disorder substantially; no clear understanding of the causal

mechanisms that produce the association between mental disorder and violence currently exits. (Silver, 2006, p. 686)

It seems that research does supports that there is, at the most, a modest connection between mental illness and the risk of violence.

It could be argued that, because a major mental disorder is only a modest risk factor for the occurrence of violence, reducing mental disorder might not substantially lessen potential violence toward society or the practitioner. To the contrary, there is seemingly greater reason to believe that changing social and personal conditions can lessen the likelihood that a mentally ill person will engage in violent conduct. Persons with mental illness tend to: (1) be poor, (2) live in impoverished conditions, and (3) be impacted by the fact that crime-prone neighborhoods increase the likelihood of violence. Coupling the downward spiral that occurs from having psychological and conduct disorders with the lack of access to supportive resources, logic supports that the typical person needing mental health services may well be more prone to end up relying on violence than the mythical "average person."

It is a fact that the mentally ill person is more apt to get in trouble with law enforcement than the mythical "average person." Law enforcement officers commonly are the first responders when there is a crisis involving a mentally disturbed person, and they have three choices: "(1) transport the person to a psychiatric facility, (2) arrest the person, or (3) resolve the matter on the spot" (Bartol & Bartol, 2012, p. 52). Citing Teplin (1986, 2000), the Bartols add: "The research on this issue finds the police try to resolve the problem on the spot 72 percent of the time, make an arrest 16 percent of the time, and initiate emergency hospitalization 12 percent of the time" (p. 52).

Some mental health advocates are chagrined about law enforcement officers being the source of interventions for mentally disordered persons. These critics believe that society has moved to criminalizing, not treating, mental illness. Placement data support this accusation. The decrease in mental health facilities and services, with no substantial change on the horizon, will likely mean that there will be increased reliance on incarceration.

For the last several decades, there has been a trend for many (most? all?) communities to reduce the availability of mental health services. With decreased funding, there has been minimal effort to go beyond use of medications for treating the chronically mentally ill.

An involuntary admission to one of the scarce beds in a mental hospital depends upon an expert predicting imminent violence by the person. Given the financial cost of in-patient treatment and the fact that research shows that mental health professionals' predictions of violence may be no better than chance (recall the issues of clinical versus statistical or actuarial methods), current public policy strongly opposes in-patient services. Whether a voluntary or involuntary admission, if the person is admitted to an in-patient placement and is not promptly violent, the person is likely to be returned to the community.

For essentially everyone, stressful life events may increase the likelihood of violence. Bad social relationships elevate stress and, consequently, the potential for violence. Under stress, a person may experience negative emotional or affective states, such as anger, fear, and frustration, which, in turn, might lead to inept "corrective actions," that is, violent behavior.

Some service users may be prone to demonstrate "psychological reactance," which is:

> A model stating that in response to a perceived threat to or loss of a behavioral freedom a person will experience psychological reactance (or, more simply, reactance), a motivational state characterized by distress, anxiety, resistance, and the desire to restore the freedom. According to this model, when people feel coerced or forced into a certain behavior, they will react against the coercion, often by demonstrating an increased preference for the behavior that is restrained and may perform the opposite behavior to that desired. (VandenBos, 2007, p. 771)

If the person has delusional beliefs or hallucinations, well-intentioned attempts to inhibit or dissuade the mentally ill person from the disturbing behavior may be met with aggression. Mentally disordered people believe that aggression and violent behavior are means for goal achievement or retribution against the cause of the person's problems—the real or symbolic source is attacked. Studies of the mentally ill who are violent have revealed high levels of stress.

The lack of adequate in-patient or other types of community mental health services means that problems are elevated for the mentally ill person and society. Persons who previously would have been in a protective treatment placement or program are now left to fend for themselves, and their mental status may make them vulnerable to adverse influences. With the futility of coping effectively with the stresses and strains of everyday life, the person in need of mental health services is more apt to resort to violence and create victims or, conversely, become a victim of violence. Stated bluntly, increasing the availability for treatment for mental disorders and improving the conditions in which the person lives would lessen violence.

Before moving past the issue of management of risk of dangerousness, it should be underscored that mental health practitioners must be on the lookout for short-term events (i.e., a transition, such as getting married, having a child) that may be a positive or a negative in the service user's life. A transition may lead to more ego strength or introduce additional stress.

A person usually seeks mental health services due to stress. Certainly stressful events, such as being terminated from employment, arrested, failing in school, getting a divorce, death of a family member or friend, or illness (self or loved ones), can lead to a need for mental health services. Therefore, monitoring for disruptive or stressful events is a major part of risk management.

A service user experiencing draining or overwhelming anxiety, frustration, or confusion needs a mental health practitioner to provide empathic understanding and support, facilitate self-understanding, and offer guidance for acquiring improved coping skills. To deal with stress effectively, the service user needs to move along a positive long-term pathway through life. Said simply, a positive trajectory contradicts aggression and violence, and fosters health, happiness, and productivity.

VIOLENCE BY MENTAL HEALTH SERVICE USERS

All mentally ill, emotionally disturbed, and behaviorally disordered persons are not necessarily going to be hostile-aggressive or violent. That said, psychological burdens potentially increase the risk of inappropriate aggression.

There are two questions to consider: (1) Do psychological and conduct problems lead to mental illness?; (2) Are mental health practitioners under more risk of assaultive or violent behavior from service users today than in past years? Regrettably, the logical answer for each of the two questions is yes.

The previous discussion in this chapter on the causes of aggression and violence pointed out how tolerance for stress is a major issue. Although research does not establish a strong link between needing mental health services and violence, there is face validity for believing that a person who needs professional mental health services senses or acts in a way that reflects poor or inadequate life-management skills. Acquiring more effective life-management skills is a major reason why many service users seek professional interventions.

In regard to the second question, the demise of community mental health services and treatment facilities and the commercial conveyance of violence in the mass or popular media certainly create greater vulnerability to stress and increased awareness of use of aggression and violence as a way of dealing with stressful conflicts and problems. Based on data from the Bureau of Labor Statistics, Bartol and Bartol (2012) indicate that the top six occupations for risk of violence are (in order): (1) police officers, (2) correctional officers, (3) taxi drivers, (4) private security guards, (5) bartenders, and (6) mental health professionals.

Setting aside taxi drivers and bartenders, it may be assumed that police officers, correctional officers, and private security guards are trained mentally and physically to deal with dangerous persons. The same, of course, cannot be said about mental health professionals.

As previously mentioned, training to be a mental health practitioner emphasizes communicating unconditional positive regard to the service user. This lack of training leaves the practitioner vulnerable to violent attack. As will be discussed further in Chapter Nine, personal defensiveness is an honorable quality for modern mental health practitioners. (Anecdotal information indicates that taxi drivers and bartenders often have a firearm readily available.)

Assaultive behavior against therapists seemed limited until the late 1960s; by the mid-1970s, about 80 percent of mental health professionals encountered at least one dangerous person per year, about 40 percent felt threatened, and about 25 percent (or a bit less) had been assaulted. Guy, Brown, and Poelstra (1990) surveyed psychologists and found: "A total of 39.9 percent . . . reported having been attacked on one or more occasions, and 49 percent indicated that they had been verbally threatened with physical attack" (p. 493). Also, about 33 percent of mental health practitioners did not list their home address in the phone book, about 20 percent avoided working alone in the office, 13 percent (by 1990) had home alarms, 5 percent kept a weapon at home, and 2 percent kept a weapon at the office.

More recently, Pope and Vasquez (2011) surveyed the literature about the stalking, threatening, and attacking of psychologists by service users. They summarize that, relevant to psychologists, about 20 percent have been attacked by at least one client; 80 percent are afraid of being attacked; 50 percent have fantasies of being attacked; 25 percent have sought police or security protection; and 3 percent have a weapon for protection. Their Web site (http://kspope.com/stalking.php) offers additional information, including a reference list of resources. (Note: Anecdotal information suggests that, since training in firearms includes the principle "Don't ask, don't tell" about ownership of a firearm, it seems likely that gun ownership is substantially higher.)

Why would a mental health practitioner become a target? Meloy (1992) indicates that in assaults in general, the attacker views the victim as threatening the attacker's ego structure, and uses a hostile action to reduce the threat and thereby creates intrapsychic homeostasis. Thus, if a person becomes uncomfortable with another person, the coercive power relationship between the two people will presumably determine whether anxiety or anger will be experienced. It is less distressing to externalize anger than to be anxious, and the angry person becomes the "active agent," who appears to be influencing and controlling the other person (the victim).

When there is a power struggle for control of the marital relationship, it seems that there is a substantial increase in threats received and concern about personal safety.

When the mental health practitioner accesses or intrudes into the mind of the mentally fragile person, even though it is to help, some service users will transform this push to gain psychological insight and behavioral change into being a threat to the ego structure. Consequently, the practitioner becomes the target of aggression and hostility.

From my experience, I believe that one of the most risky areas of mental health practice is working with families. When there is a power struggle for control of the marital relationship, it seems that there is a substantial increase in threats received and concern about personal safety. Among domestic or family attorneys, it is well known that threats are common in divorce cases, especially when there are custody-related issues. For example, it is not unusual for a divorcing spouse to punch in drywall or a paper-thin door, or to make a death threat against the other spouse's attorney. The mental health practitioner providing marriage and family therapy seemingly has the same elevated risk. Because a divorce cuts to the heart of self-esteem and personal security, this risk can even come from a divorcing spouse with a previous record of mental strength.

The primary message is that mental health practitioners need to adopt a reality-based view of the possibility of violence. Nurturance and altruism must not blind the practitioner to the threat of violence.

PSYCHOLOGICAL TRIGGERS FOR VIOLENCE

In keeping with threat assessment, the mental health practitioner should be aware of the psychological conditions that may lead a service user to act in an aggressive and violent manner. There are two basic conditions that the practitioner should continually assess: (1) the service user's ego system, and (2) any change in the equilibrium in the service user's life.

The client with a weak or struggling ego system is vulnerable to stress that could be overwhelming and lead to aggressive communications and violent behavior. One behavior to look for is resistance to mental health treatment, which a client may use as a means to preserve ego functioning and stability. A proliferation or escalation of reliance on ego defense mechanisms is a warning sign of aggressive or violent behavior. Consider how each of the following mechanisms could be demonstrated:

- Autism—To substitute fantasy for fact to defend self-esteem against feelings of inadequacy or failure; to avoid reality by delusion.
- Compensation—To substitute one activity for another to accommodate frustrated motives; to counterbalance a problem by success in another area; to offset a weakness with a strength.
- Defensive Devaluation—To emphasize the weaknesses or problems of others in order to ward off recognition of one's own deficiencies.
- Displacement—To camouflage the goal of a motive by placing another in its stead; to direct aggression on to a source other than the cause of agitation.
- Identification—To become ego-involved with persons or things to defend against feelings of inadequacy or weakness; to view oneself as being the same as or part of some person or competency, power, or high status.
- Isolation—To withdraw from contact with problem sources; to avoid having to deal with conflicts by staying out of their reach.

- Projection—To avoid a conflict by attributing one's own motives, thoughts, or weaknesses to someone else.
- Rationalization—To find a reason to justify an action or position; to use an excuse to make the irrational seem rational; to accept a substitute motive.
- Reaction Formation—To disguise a motive that is unacceptable or unpleasant by expressing it or behaving in a manner directly opposite from its original intent.
- Regression—To retreat to primitive or less mature behavior; to resolve frustration though avoiding responsibility.
- Repression—To not allow memories or motives into consciousness (but they continue to operate at the unconscious level); to put unpleasant things out of your mind.
- Undoing—To achieve symbolic restitution for a past or present impulse, thought, or behavior that is considered to be unacceptable; to assure irrationally that another deed can wipe away a negative.

These defense mechanisms are typical for persons needing mental health services. However, when any one of these defense mechanisms escalates during the course of treatment, the risk of illogical decisions about how to deal with stress will begin to emerge. Inadequate coping with stress can lead to the chaining that results in frustration, disappointment, aggravation, aggression, hostility, and violence.

VIOLENCE IN THE MENTAL HEALTH SERVICES CONTEXT

The very nature of professional mental health services means that the service user is not functioning in a healthy way. There is a sense of inadequacy to cope with one's problems in life, and help is sought from another person, such as a mental health practitioner.

The very nature of professional mental health services means that the service user is not functioning in a healthy way. There is a sense of inadequacy to cope with one's problems in life, and help is sought from another person, such as a mental health practitioner.

In searching for help to relieve the chaining of frustration, disappointment, aggravation, aggression, hostility, and violence, some service users target a helpful source. That is, they displace their negative emotions

116

and faulty reasoning onto the helper (e.g., a mental health practitioner). The ego defense mechanisms described earlier may exemplify how negative conditions, not justified by the reality of the relationship, may result in blaming a support source.

When a potential support source is blamed and victimized, the offender is experiencing dyscontrol, which may be conceived as the ultimate trigger for violence. Several decades ago, Elliott (1977) posited "episodic dyscontrol syndrome," which linked the dyscontrol to a bodily reaction to chronic stress. It also is known as Intermittent Explosive Disorder (*DSM-IV* 312.34), for which the diagnostic criteria are:

1. Several discrete episodes of failure to resist aggressive impulses that result in serious assaultive acts or destruction of property.
2. The degree of aggressiveness expressed during the episodes is grossly out of proportion to any precipitating psychosocial stressors.
3. The aggressive episodes are not better accounted for by another mental disorder (e.g., Antisocial Personality Disorder, Borderline Personality Disorder, a Psychotic Disorder, a Manic Episode, Conduct Disorder, or Attention-Deficit/Hyperactivity Disorder) and are not due to the direct physiological effects of a substance (e.g., a drug of abuse, a medication) or a general medical condition (e.g., head trauma, Alzheimer's disease). (American Psychiatric Association, 1994, p. 612)

There are other impulse control problems contained in the *DSM-IV* and more are apt to be added in future editions of the *DSM*. As stated, impulse control problems result in aggressiveness grossly out of proportion to the actual precipitating psychosocial stressor, and cannot be accounted for by any mental disorder per se.

Analyses of risks in the context of a professional service relationship reveals that there are 10 "profiles" or personality disorders that provide a significant risk of violence to the mental health practitioner. Note that these 10 types of behavioral styles are on a continuum of introversion-extraversion. Also, several, if not all, of these profiles have a distinct psychopathic dimension (Babiak & Hare, 2006).

1. **The Downtrodden.** These people commonly present themselves as being victimized, whether by the world at large or particular persons.

Even if they have social, financial, and family support systems, they want others to believe that they have no reasonable chance of survival or success, and in some instances, they believe that others should have no expectations of them or should make sacrifices for them. If dyscontrol occurs, this mindset includes thoughts of committing desperate acts, such as crimes. Abuse, assault, suicide, or homicide can result.

2. **The Shadow**. These people tend to avoid contact with others, even members of their own families, work colleagues, and previous friends and acquaintances. They try to stay in the background, keeping their thoughts private and behaviors masked or camouflaged. The loneliness associated with this behavioral style can fuel notions of striking out at anyone who is believed to be infringing on their compulsive efforts to maintain personal privacy.

3. **The Fiddler**. Due to these people's inner world of self-doubts and unmet needs, there will be episodic or continuous frenetic attempts to change or manipulate the outer world, namely the way that others respond to their expressed wishes. Failure to elicit the desired responses, such as compliance by or support from others, can lead to agitation, and movement into the violence chain.

4. **The Encroacher**. These people invade others' rights and privacy in order to bolster a flagging ego and construct a false sense of power and control to wrest away others' resources. There is no *quid pro quo*; that is, if the other person is pulled into the world of the Encroacher, there will still be a negative response, which can become violent. Likewise, if the person encroached on resists giving up resources, the chain of violence will occur. For the victim(s), it is a no-win situation.

5. **The Volcano**. These people have an inner fire of insecurity and inadequacy that brings the emotional caldron to a boil, and violence overflows—in contradiction to the person's usual emotionally dormant demeanor. This is the explosive personality that is so common in domestic and workplace violence situations. If watched carefully, the surface behavior is usually not placid; there are bubbles of inappropriate behavior that reveal the chain of violence. However, just like Mount Saint Helens, when the eruption occurs, extreme destruction can be expected.

6. **The Great Pretender**. Psychopathy, rooted in maladaptive self-aggrandizement, leads these people to present false information and

attempt to seduce others (in the broad sense of "seduction"). Among other things, they may pretend to be super-moral and hold impeccable values, when they are really primed for intemperance, debauchery, and asocial/antisocial actions; hardworking (and high achieving) when they really believe that they should be exempt from personal labor and others should fulfill their needs; and greatly impressed with another person (e.g., "you are definitely the most impressive person whom I have ever met"), but when the person has satisfied or failed to satisfy the relevant needs, the Great Pretender will turn on the person forcefully and with anger. This behavioral style is the *sine qua non* of the psychopath and sociopath.

7. **The Majestic**. These people, much like the Great Pretender, with roots in extreme narcissism, live with a profound sense of entitlement. For magically derived reasons, they believe that they are "titleholders," and everyone else should recognize their superiority and that they should not have to act in a responsible fashion on a continuous basis. Here again, there is a direct connection to psychopathy and sociopathy.

8. **The Cobra**. Like their deadly namesake, these people generally avoid others, but when there is direct or indirect contact that creates uneasiness or fear, they move into position, coiled and ready to strike. They may attempt to deceive others by mesmerizing moves. Their victims may have unintentionally crossed their paths. With a framework of self-protection, being threatened (which may be an irrational fear) leads them to strike out with deadly impact.

9. **The Rat**. These people completely disrespect the rights of others. They scurry around everywhere (e.g., the community) devouring anything or anyone that seems to offer gratification, albeit unearned or undeserved. There is no respect for any personal or social convention. Sociopathy leads to blatant criminal behavior, which can readily be destructive and violent.

10. **The Tyrant**. These people are on a quest for arbitrary, unrestrained, and absolute rule, often cruel and oppressive. Others are expected to be unquestioning, conforming, and obedient. Resistance to or rejection of the dictates can trigger volatility.

There can be permutations of each of these 10 profiles of high-risk people. When any of the characteristics of these profiles becomes evident, the prudent mental health practitioner should promptly initiate professional efforts to reduce the risk and prevent the manifestation of any sort of hostile or violent act. Certainly the mental health practitioner should not let any hostility disrupt the professional mental health service relationship. For example, the noncompliance that is within each of these profiles makes it foolhardy to attempt to continue treatment; the chances of successful behavior change are minimal, unless there is a well-structured intervention regime and milieu (Babiak & Hare, 2006).

Beyond violence per se, a service user with any of the foregoing characteristics (even a partial fulfillment of one of the 10 profiles), especially one with a narcissistic and/or psychopathic bent, should be considered a prime candidate for eventually filing an ethics or licensing complaint or lawsuit against a mental health practitioner.

CONCLUSION

For modern mental health practice, the assessment of risks and threats is required. Social learning influences a person's reliance on aggression. Mental health professionals are at risk of stalking, threats, and attacks by services users; safety measures against this violence toward the mental health professional are justified. Chapter Nine provides information about how practitioners can maintain appropriate defensiveness against threats and violence.

NINE

Appropriate Defensiveness

Throughout the earlier chapters of this book, the thesis has been that mental health practitioners must ensure quality care, but also must be wary of negative responses from service users. Emphasis has been placed on not allowing risks to develop, which means that there cannot be carte blanche deference to the service user. Quality care and risk management benefit society, the service user, and the practitioner. Given society's requirement that professional services be qualitatively solid, neither the service user nor the practitioner should accept conditions that could jeopardize quality care or infringe on the personal or legal rights of anyone.

This chapter sets forth information and guidelines for insulating the mental health practitioner from risks, providing information about an appropriate defensive mindset, personal defense strategies, defining the professional service context, interactions with service users, and structuring the office setup. With all

With all due respect, any professor, member of an ethics committee or licensing board, government regulator, attorney, or another health care professional who is critical of mental health practitioners' preserving personal rights or requiring service users to adhere to professional standards is operating by an antiquated or misguided mindset.

due respect, any professor, member of an ethics committee or licensing board, government regulator, attorney, or another health care professional who is critical of mental health practitioners' preserving personal rights or requiring service users to adhere to professional standards is operating by an antiquated or misguided mindset.

DEFENSIVENESS MINDSET

To deal effectively with risk from threats, danger, and violence, the mental health practitioner must be physically and mentally fit for the challenges. Foremost is the mindset. Basically, the practitioner should cultivate realistic confidence and be able and ready to implement appropriate actions. Being a mental health practitioner does not require sacrificing any personal or legal rights, such as the right of privacy. If a service user or anyone else threatens or abuses the mental health practitioner, there must be immediate personal defensiveness.

Late one afternoon, I received a frantic telephone call from a practitioner asking "What do I do? A client has barged into my partner's office, knocked him down, and is on top of him and beating on him—I can't call the police because of confidentiality." With all due respect for such a naïve belief, if there is ever any threat of violence, disregard other options and call law enforcement.

Whether dealing with a social contact or a service user, the mental health practitioner should not throw caution to the wind. To the contrary, there is ample reason for a practitioner to constantly be processing information for any nuance of risk—surveillance for adverse conditions supports both quality care and risk management.

In any relationship, neither verbal nor physical abuse should be tolerated. In mental health services, the abusive person destroys the "therapeutic alliance" or "professional relationship." If abuse (which would include threats) happens, the mental health practitioner should move expediently into preserving personal rights and self-protection. Decisive protective actions are justified.

Regardless of the relationship, a threatening or abusive person must not be allowed to gain control. When there is a cloud of threat and potential violence, trying to "talk the attacker down" is foolhardy. Being a passive recipient of abuse or violence is not an option under any circumstance.

When a service user seems agitated and on the verge of possible assaultive conduct, the mental health practitioner should literally and figuratively use distance as a protection. In other words, the practitioner should move back. Among other things, distance allows for a highly effective defensive strategy—flight.

When learning any new skill, such as how to use a particular software program, the professional diligently studies a manual, signs up for classes, or arranges for tutoring. Mental health practitioners should use the same tools for learning to protect themselves and their professional services; practitioners should consult an attorney, train in personal protection, or learn martial arts.

One of the first thoughts about self-defense is to have a firearm. Anyone can learn to discharge a gun, but proper and effective use requires mental training as well as safety training. Various people have told me that, even though they own a gun, they could never shoot anyone, no matter what was occurring. Those people should not have a firearm. On the other hand, there is no reason why a mental health practitioner with proper training should not legally have a firearm for personal protection. Informal surveys indicate that more mental health practitioners have a handgun than has been published. For example, on one mental health ethics committee, five of eight members owned a handgun.

An important component of a protective mindset is the axiom: If violence is unavoidable, do what it takes. The mental health practitioner should capitalize on surprise, fight dirty, use simple maneuvers, expect to win, and not worry about ego or criticism after the fact. Without self-preservation, the mental health practitioner will be a sacrificial lamb for psychopathology and conduct disorders.

PERSONAL DEFENSE STRATEGIES

Being a mental health practitioner does not require sacrificing any personal or legal rights. Although this principle is applicable to a myriad of legally based rights, foremost is the Constitutionally based right to privacy.

Every mental health practitioner should create a "zone of privacy" for personal living. The social responsibility and legal duty to a service user ends at the perimeter of the professional service context. No service user should be allowed into the zone of personal privacy, during or after the provision of services.

One practitioner was shocked to find a client (with a borderline personality) standing in the living room. The client explained, "I told the guard at the gate that we went to high school together and I wanted to surprise you." Reaching the house, the client had told the practitioner's elementary school children the same thing, and was admitted into the house.

The foregoing borderline client was known to have violent propensities. This sort of intrusion into the practitioner's home constituted a clear breach of the policies relevant to inappropriate multiple relations and the definition of the service relationship—which should be stated orally and in writing at the outset of professional services.

Part of maintaining an appropriate individualized treatment plan is to require compliance by the service user. When a client violates clearly defined limits, there should be no opportunity for a subsequent breach. The practitioner should terminate permanently any service user who intrudes into the zone of personal privacy—no exceptions.

Part of maintaining an appropriate individualized treatment plan is to require compliance by the service user. When a client violates clearly defined limits, there should be no opportunity for a subsequent breach. The practitioner should terminate permanently any service user who intrudes into the zone of personal privacy—no exceptions.

It is almost impossible to keep one's home address out of public information. Recognizing the potential for danger, some jurisdictions allow judges, attorneys, and law enforcement personnel to keep home addresses off of public documents, including vehicle registrations, driver's licenses, etc. Mental health practitioners should have this same protection, but unfortunately it does not seem to be forthcoming at this time. However, the mental health practitioner should try to minimize public access to personal contact information as much as possible. The threshold action is to not have a home telephone number or address listed anywhere, unless legally required.

The Internet makes it difficult to keep personal information private, and has introduced new avenues for accessing personal information about a mental health practitioner. Aside from sites presumably for promoting practices, there are numerous search engines and sites that will reveal personal details, including residence. Moreover, social networks (such as Facebook) are fertile for personal information. Even if a service user is not admitted to a list of "friends," surreptitious means—a bogus name—can be used to obtain some personal information about a practitioner.

As a rule of thumb, a mental health practitioner should routinely check search engines, and when it is discovered that personal information appears, steps should be taken to get the information removed. The practitioner should not post or allow any personal information on the Web (including on a social network) that the practitioner does not want the world, figuratively and literally, to know now and forever. When a "practice promotion" site contains personal information, steps should be taken to remove it.

A practitioner should never give out a home or cell phone; to do so, is opening the door to intrusions. Legally, a mental health practitioner is not required to be "on call" 24 hours a day, 7 days a week. This is certainly true for independent practitioners (as opposed to a mental health clinic or hospital). All that is necessary is to provide service users with a proper authoritative source for emergencies. For example, on a telephonic message state: "In case of emergency, please contact 911 or go to your nearest emergency center." This statement also should appear in the written policies given to every client from the outset of services. Providing every client with the limits of availability and contact information for an emergency (such as a local crisis center) should be sufficient. Too many practitioners seem to reveal a self-aggrandizing element when they make themselves unnecessarily available.

It is well worth the cost of a post office box in order to keep one's home address confidential. As a mental health practitioner, never assume that a service user will not be ingenious in a pathological pursuit of intruding into your personal life. For example, a practitioner wanted to avoid a lawsuit and moved out of town with no forwarding address. The plaintiff's attorney simply waited a few weeks and had another practitioner in the same discipline obtain the new address from the membership records for the relevant national professional association.

The instructor at a seminar, a senior law enforcement officer, was bragging about how no one could locate his home address. In the course of the presentation, the presenter mentioned having a spouse who was a mental health practitioner. During the noon hour, a participant used the Internet to check the membership directory for the primary professional association with which the spouse was affiliated. When the seminar reconvened, the instructor was taken aback when told that the spouse's listing in a particular professional directory contained both the home address and telephone number.

Contrary to the notion of "personalizing" an office to make a service user feel more at home, protecting the rights of and minimizing risks to the mental health practitioner justifies keeping the office attractive but spartan. All personal items, including family pictures, should be removed from the office. With all due respect, a practitioner who does otherwise is being naïve or revealing a bit of narcissism. By this time, it almost goes without saying, that the mental health practitioner should always be alert to personal risk, danger, and/or violence. If the situation does not feel safe, it probably is not safe.

One mental health practitioner was just wrapping up a long day of seeing clients. It was about 9:00 p.m. and the office building was basically empty. While turning off lights, the practitioner became aware that someone was in the waiting room. It turned out to be a male, who explained that he was looking for what was obviously a fictitious business. Fortunately the stranger left. The next day, the practitioner was treating a rape victim who said, "Let me show you a picture of my ex-boyfriend who raped me." It was the same fellow who had been in the waiting room the night before. The practitioner immediately entered into self-defense classes. The firearms instructor advised that, when leaving the office alone at night, the practitioner should always have a loaded pistol.

Part of a good personal defense is being able to detect the danger. When alone, even in seemingly safe places, the mental health practitioner should stay focused on what is occurring. It is wise to carry a cell phone at all times with critical numbers on automatic dial.

Part of a good personal defense is being able to detect the danger. A good practice is to have an ultra-bright flashlight in every vehicle and every room in the office and at home. If the lights go out or there is an unexplained sound, having to go to another room and rummage around in search of a flashlight could be futile. When alone, even in seemingly safe places, the mental health practitioner should stay focused on what is occurring. It is wise to carry a cell phone at all times with critical numbers on automatic dial.

A female practitioner was jogging in daylight at 7:00 a.m. in a small town public park. There were passing cars on a street within 15 feet. Prior to waking up in a creek with an assailant beating her with a rock, the last thing that she remembered was her headset saying, "This is your favorite radio station and it is 7:00 a.m." She barely survived, and the assailant was never caught. The point of the preceding example is that having a headset distracted her from detecting any warning sounds or signs (as might have allowed her to escape or to defend herself). It was also foolish to think, because it was a small town, a public park, daylight, and a public roadway was nearby that it was safe.

In this day and age, a mental health practitioner cannot afford to not have an electronic home security system—and must use it. Given the high risk of being a mental health practitioner, an electronic security system for both home and office should be considered "part of the cost of doing business."

Just like thinking that that a small town public park in daylight is safe, it is foolish to think that residing in a seemingly low crime neighborhood has no risk of a burglary or home invasion. Despite being in an upscale neighborhood, one mental health practitioner, working alone one morning in the home office (with the outer doors locked), suddenly sensed that there was someone at her shoulder. A male, with a gun, knocked the practitioner to the floor, stole jewelry and other things, and escaped. Thankfully practitioner's physical injuries were not severe, but the traumatic effects are continuing years later. There had been a home security system, but the practitioner did not use it during the day and was ill-prepared for self-defense.

When the mental health practitioner is trained for the proper and safe use of firearms, the weapon needs to be readily available. When issuing concealed weapon permits, one law enforcement officer sermonizes, "An unloaded pistol is a bigger risk than not having a pistol—keep it loaded at all times." Given the quickness of an assault, any weapon, including a firearm, has to be operable and obtainable within seconds.

One person bought a starter pistol (which does not shoot ammunition, only blanks) to carry concealed. This person stated: "I assume that if anyone tried to attack me, I can scare them away with my fake gun." Perhaps ignorance is bliss, but it certainly offers no protection. In fact, having a real or fake gun that cannot be used immediately and with confidence might actually incite the attacker to greater violence.

A person who carries a gun but believes "I could never shoot anyone" is increasing the risks, not lessening them. The person who is well trained in the use of deadly force knows that the mindset for use of a weapon of any kind is of critical importance. If one cannot mentally implement an appropriate defense, there will be disaster.

Another mental health practitioner scoffed at the idea of home security. When asked how he or she would defend young children in the household from a home invasion, he or she said, "It wouldn't happen in my neighborhood, but if it did, I would get my baseball bat." When asked where the bat was kept, the practitioner confessed "I have no idea where it is." It takes only seven or eight sections to do a forced entry into a home!

Obviously, naiveté or a commitment to nonviolence does not justify a lack of protection. One mental health practitioner (a personal friend of mine), who had spoken publicly against firearms, was shot and killed by a mentally disordered person.

Another mental health practitioner sensed something was wrong with the home security system, so had the security company check the premises. They found that a sophisticated alteration to the electronic notification of law enforcement had been done (wiring had been changed). It was clear that it was not due to the installation. Although never proven, it appeared that one of the practitioner's former "romantic" friends, who had a record of domestic abuse, was the cause of the malfunction in the security system. One can only speculate about what might have been the former friend's underlying intentions. Incidentally, the practitioner had broken off the social relationship with the former friend because of what was sensed to be a risk of violence. Living alone in a rural area, the practitioner received training for the use of firearms, and now keeps a loaded pump shotgun and an ultra-bright flashlight next to the bed.

Somewhat similarly, a practitioner was in the midst of divorcing an abusive spouse. During a pre-arranged visit, the spouse asked for some business papers; the practitioner said, "I'll need a few minutes, they are in the file cabinet in the back room, just wait here in the living room." When hearing about the incident, the practitioner's attorney suggested checking the living room; a listening device was found to have been installed behind an electric socket plate.

Because mental health practitioners are not usually trained to deal with threats and violence, it is wise to obtain the services of a security consultant. There may be alternatives that will be better than the existing protection for the zone of personal privacy.

DEFINING THE SERVICE CONTEXT

From the outset of professional services, the mental health practitioner should let all potential service users and significant others know that there is "zero tolerance" for any indicator of potential violence. This information should be provided orally and in writing. Even a small mental health practice should have a workplace violence policy.

The mental health practitioner must develop a set of techniques for de-escalation of tension that starts to build in anyone who is on the premises. Mental health practitioners are prone to want to "talk it out," but when dealing with an irrational, threatening person, this could be foolhardy—even deadly.

From the outset of professional services, the mental health practitioner should let all potential service users and significant others know that there is "zero tolerance" for any indicator of potential violence. This information should be provided orally and in writing. Even a small mental health practice should have a workplace violence policy.

When a threat is evident, the prudent thing to do is to rely on those designated by society with the authority to deal with threats: law enforcement personnel. Relevant law enforcement agencies should be on speed-dial on every office phone. When scheduled to provide services to a person charged with a crime, one mental health practitioner arranges for a deputy sheriff (usually in plain clothes) to be in the waiting room. Even if security services must be obtained for a fee, it should be viewed, regrettably, as yet another "cost of doing business" in this era.

It is useful to establish a personal connection with one or more law enforcement officers. I have found that most law enforcement officers will give their cell phone numbers to mental health practitioners for 24/7 contact.

The mental health practitioner should have a competent attorney in place for filing and obtaining an *ex parte* order of protection, or taking any other action that may require legal expertise. Numerous practitioners have described situations in which a service user has made dozens of telephone calls, leaving a message each time, or stalked the practitioner (e.g., sitting in an automobile in front of the practitioner's office or home in order to be seen by the practitioner). The nefarious objective is definitely to harass and intimidate. An order of protection ensures that, if there is a violation of the order by the service user, the mental health practitioner will receive the utmost action by law enforcement, because the violation is viewed as being disrespectful to the judicial and law enforcement systems.

At the first incidence of even a slightly inappropriate contact, the mental health practitioner should make an emphatic statement to the person that it must not happen again. If there is a major infringement, such as using subterfuge to gain entry into the practitioner's zone of personal privacy, it should be reported to law enforcement and there should be no further contact with the violator except through an attorney or law enforcement officer—again, no exceptions. Here is an example of the effectiveness of taking action early: After several telephone contacts by a former service user, the mental health practitioner spotted the person driving in the practitioner's neighborhood. At the suggestion of an attorney, the practitioner wisely contacted the sheriff's office, and a detective soon did an "intervention" that dissuaded the would-be suitor from any further attempted contact with the mental health practitioner.

When an employee or service user is terminated, the risk of violence escalates. When terminating a chief executive of a mental health organization, the board of directors was concerned about the potential for volatility. Arrangements were made for the termination session to be held in a conference room just off a hotel lobby, with a law enforcement officer in plain clothes sitting outside the door, looking like a guest reading the newspaper. Because each termination scenario is unique, careful planning should preface the notice of the termination.

Every mental health context or program should operate by policies that give realistic and effective protection to service users, employees, and practitioners. These policies need to be grounded in the legal rights of all concerned.

For example, in an evening session with a parent and son, the mental health practitioner became aware of noises coming through the wall, meaning that someone unexpected had entered the room next door. The parent and practitioner went to the door, but the intruder had locked it from the inside. Law enforcement was called. An unknown male, presumably with criminal intent, had made an unauthorized entry, and was arrested. Subsequently, the practitioner installed a combination lock on the outer door and instructed current service users in the extant combination code to be punched for entry (the code is changed periodically).

In a community mental health clinic, a mental health practitioner was receiving death threats from a former service user. At another clinic in the past, the same service user had been arrested for death threats against her previous practitioner. The naïve director of the community mental health clinic forbid the current practitioner from contacting law enforcement or getting an order of protection, saying, "Other patients will find out and it will be bad publicity." Upon receiving copies of the death threats, as the practitioner's attorney, I set up an emergency meeting with the county attorneys who immediately ordered the clinic director to implement certain protective measures, including filing charges against the service user, and providing the practitioner with funding for training in self protection and a secure parking place. The threatening former service user was arrested, convicted, and incarcerated.

INTERACTIONS WITH SERVICE USERS

Adopting appropriate defensiveness does not impair the professional relationship between the mental health practitioner and the service user. It merely gives added assurance for quality care and risk management, which yields appropriate benefits to society, the service user, and the practitioner.

> *Adopting appropriate defensiveness does not impair the professional relationship between the mental health practitioner and the service user. It merely gives added assurance for quality care and risk management, which yields appropriate benefits to society, the service user, and the practitioner.*

Professionalism supports treating everyone with respect and dignity, but it does not require subservience or denigration of personal or legal rights or violation of professional standards and policies. Would-be service users should be screened for appropriateness for the particular service context. Also, the needs of the service user must be compatible with the practitioner's competency.

As part of the intake process and the orientation to the practice context (prior to formal acceptance of the person for ongoing professional services), the practitioner should make it clear that the first X-number of sessions are for evaluation for suitability for ongoing professional services. The preferred theory for intervention does not bypass this requirement. The practitioner should be prepared to reject or terminate anyone who may be unduly aggressive or resistant, abusive, or violent. The professional justification for rejection or termination is simple: A service user must demonstrate a willingness and ability to conform to the policies and rules, including an appropriate individualized treatment plan. In other words, each service user must be "suitable" for, that is, will benefit from, the sort of services provided by the particular practitioner.

At the outset of and throughout services, every service user should be asked direct questions about high-risk topics, such as history of impulse control, threats, danger, and violence. There should be no hesitancy to ask for details about any arrest or conviction or the availability of weapons. Because there could be changes in the service user's psychological and conduct factors, the risk assessment should be ongoing.

Objective assessment strategies, such as psychometric measures of violence-related factors or characteristics are important. Assessment information about potential violence should be included in formal diagnoses. Any mention (even joking) or sign of potential violence toward self or others is a serious matter.

Comprehensive records of the professional communications and services facilitate risk assessment and case management. The practitioner should keep detailed records of all contacts (including telephone contacts), and not shy away from listing negative observations, even if it might be against the client's legal interests in litigation. The guideline for the contents of clinical records is to include any information that is potentially relevant and material to the goals and objectives of professional services, currently or in the future.

As has been said repeatedly throughout this book, modern mental health services require an individualized treatment plan. It must be conveyed consistently to the client that the practitioner has an ethical responsibility and legal duty to provide services according to a reasonable individualized treatment plan and the client's *quid pro quo* responsibility and duty is to be compliant with the plan and to make payment for the professional services. Noncompliant services users should be terminated permanently (referral may be necessary).

The communications and interactions between the practitioner and the service user must always be respectful and professional. The mental health practitioner should never discuss the practitioner's personal life or family members with a service user. The practitioner and the client must maintain strict boundaries. Contrary to outmoded humanistic notions, there should be no intimate sharing (no touching, not even a "therapeutic hug") (Corley, 2010). The practitioner should be wary of any seductive, ingratiating, or "niceness" messages. In this postmodern era, government regulations and legal liability do not accommodate humanistic notions.

In every contact, the mental health practitioner must be focused on professional goals and objectives; being distracted or preoccupied jeopardizes quality care and risk management. The practitioner should always be vigilant, constantly monitoring verbal and nonverbal behavior for possible noncompliance and unacceptable responses. Appropriate defensiveness supports the practitioner's staying one step ahead of the service user.

An evasive answer by the service user, should be viewed as a red flag by the practitioner. Any suggestion of deception or attempt at intimidation or control by the service user is also considered a negative behavior. For appropriate client management, there must be factual and honest answers to all questions potentially relevant and material to the goals and objectives, as determined by the practitioner, not by the service user—a lie, no matter how innocuous, is inexcusable.

When threats start to emerge, the practitioner should be unflappable and be an unwilling victim. The practitioner should not accept any demand from a service user that might jeopardize professionalism or personal safety. It is best not to challenge the potentially abusive person, but rather use one-downsmanship and permanently terminate all services, making a referral, if necessary.

When a threat is detected, the practitioner should immediately focus on risk management. The mental health practitioner should keep verbal responses firm, unequivocal, and brief—and mentally move to the next step of planning a defensive strategy. From the legal perspective, the threat has canceled any professional duty, so it is not "abandonment" to terminate the professional services relationship. The practitioner should not over-think the situation—a threat is a threat is a threat. As said previously stated, contacting law enforcement is often the option of choice.

STRUCTURING THE OFFICE SETUP

Obviously the physical factors for an office vary greatly. This section offers a number of suggestions, realizing that some ideas will be impossible or even inappropriate for certain physical features of the professional service context. As a caveat, there may be some offices that are unacceptable for certain mental health services as, for example, an office suite that is next door to a high-risk community agency.

The office suite needs to have protection, such as an electronic alarm system. Depending on the nature of the practice, this could have relevance both day and night. Several practitioners have had nighttime office break-ins in which files or computer hard drives were taken (the nefarious motivation is obvious). Recall some of the previously cited cases that mentioned the usefulness of an electronic security system.

Initial construction of a building seldom considers safety per se. Also, because many tenants are responsible for paying for interior partitioning, some frugal practitioners might opt for unsafe features to save money. For example, hollow doors offer virtually no resistance to a forced entry, and the typical door casings add to the vulnerability by being quite thin. The door casings or frame and the door should be strong, preferably metal. In addition, the doors should have locks that can be activated from the inside and be kept locked as much as possible (remember the practitioner working at home who was surprised by a daytime intruder).

Favor should be given to solid barriers. Glass partitions, such as in front of the receptionist, should be minimized and strengthened. There should be a one-way (small) window for seeing to the other side of a solid door. For personal safety, it may be necessary to incur expense and sacrifice aesthetic appeal.

It is always best to avoid being in the office alone and at high-risk times (remember the practitioner who had an after-hours encounter with an alleged rapist in the waiting room). Try to have at least two people in the office working at the same time, and to arrive and leave together. Likewise, it is advisable to park in a well-lit area that can be seen by passersby.

Finally, there should be no reluctance to involve law enforcement in any potentially dangerous situation. Also, the practitioner should not hesitate to request a plain-clothes law enforcement officer or security officer to be in the waiting room when a potentially dangerous service user is scheduled or when the practitioner is leaving the office.

CONCLUSION

The time has come for mental health practitioners to exercise precautionary protective measures. There is no reason to believe that appropriate defensiveness contradicts the professional relationship. To the contrary, being sure that risks, threats, danger, and violence do not disrupt the professional services promotes quality care and risk management resulting in a benefit to society, the service user, and the mental health practitioner.

Chapter Ten explores basic guidelines for defining, maintaining, and operating a mental health practice in a manner that will maximize the chances for success and avoid ethical and regulatory complaints and legal challenges. These ideas, like those for appropriate defensiveness, contribute to quality care and risk management.

Avoiding Ethical and Licensing Complaints and Legal Challenges

The rationale for risk assessment and management is two-fold: (1) quality care is maintained, and (2) the personal and the legal rights of the service user and the practitioner are honored. An appropriate concomitant objective is to avoid, or at least minimize the likelihood of, ethical and licensing complaints, as well as legal challenges (e.g., a malpractice action). Bennett et al. (2006) report that, over the previous decade, complaints to ethics committees declined, malpractice lawsuits remained at about the same level, and "the risk of a licensing board complaint has increased substantially" (p. 20). To complicate matters, training programs for mental health practitioners commonly fail to adequately prepare practitioners to maintain self-protection, risk management, and appropriate defensiveness.

This chapter presents ways for the mental health practitioner to avoid becoming a respondent in an ethics or licensing complaint or legal challenge. The focus is on professional self-concept, professional reputation, a protective practice framework, client management, and developing a "warrior" mindset. Specific suggestions are offered that lead to efficient policies and operations, and prepare the practitioner for potential adversity in the professional context. Although the structure for this approach was formulated in earlier books (Woody, 1988a, 1988b), the substantive information and ideas presented have evolved and are uniquely tailored to contemporary mental health practices.

PROFESSIONAL SELF-CONCEPT

The vast majority of people rely on employment or career for a sense of self-worth. The importance of being a professional has both a positive and a negative influence on one's self-concept. Certainly the status and income factors associated with being a mental health professional can be rewarding, but there is also the risk of others resenting or targeting the professional, especially in a society that seems to be moving toward less respect for and less trust of health care practitioners. Regrettably, because a practitioner is not exempt or immune from psychological errors, there is also the risk of poor decisions and foolish or inadvertent errors by the practitioner.

There should be no affiliation with any organization unless it has an unimpeachable track record for being committed to maintaining professional standards.

The mental health practitioner needs to adhere to professional standards, which means avoiding any service, activity, role, or job for which the practitioner does not have impeccable and well documented competency. There should be no succumbing to self-aggrandizement, such as "purchasing" a vanity credential (Woody, 1998, 2007). There should be no affiliation with any organization unless it has an unimpeachable track record for being committed to maintaining professional standards. When making a self-assessment or in communicating about competency and services to others, the mental health practitioner should harbor no notion about expertise that is not totally consonant with national and, perhaps to a lesser extent, parochial standards.

Being a mental health practitioner is demanding. The nature of the professional services inevitably impacts on and drains ego strength, yet prosocial behavior also nurtures and increases ego strength. Having said the foregoing, the mental health practitioner should avoid an isolated practice. Being able to interact with colleagues (e.g., other practitioners in the clinic) offers important protection for ego strength and, therefore, wisdom in judgments about service users. Regardless of training or experience, it is wise to maintain a supervisory relationship (the more formal the better) and seek continuing education.

It is understandable that university and professional training programs are committed to academic idealism. However, the lack of preparation for the reality of mental health practice is illogical. As a result, it is up to each mental health professional to create individualized initiatives to learn how to provide mental health professional services as a business and, regardless of the preferred theory or service context, maintain career-investment strategies that will further a long-term business-oriented practice.

As with any "battle plan," it is helpful to have allies. Protection from lawsuits and regulatory and ethics complaints calls for strong reliance on and communication with professionals outside the health care profession, particularly an attorney and an accountant who are well versed in laws and issues pertaining to the particular jurisdiction in which the mental health practice is located. It is a good investment to purchase professional liability insurance that covers not only malpractice lawsuits per se, but ethics and licensing complaints as well. Given the complexity of the issues and long duration applied to many complaints, the amount of insurance coverage for malpractice and licensing complaints should not be minimal.

> *It is a good investment to purchase professional liability insurance that covers not only malpractice lawsuits per se, but ethics and licensing complaints as well. Given the complexity of the issues and long duration applied to many complaints, the amount of insurance coverage for malpractice and licensing complaints should not be minimal.*

PROFESSIONAL REPUTATION AND OFFICE ARRANGEMENTS

There is truth and relevance in the old adage: "You are known by the company you keep." The concept of vicarious liability creates persuasive reasons for restricting and monitoring relationships with other practitioners.

Every mental health practitioner must understand and operate by economic principles. Goodheart (2010) opines that the lack of training and interest in economics "limits our ability to understand and to affect the economic factors and systems that dramatically influence the ways in which we can practice, be paid for our work, and ensure access for those in need of psychological services" (p. 189). Incidentally, Goodheart makes the point that it is not a matter of marketing, it is the fundamentals of operating a business. The future national health care system increases the need for economic knowledge, and includes "the acceleration of the accountability movement, the shrinking portion of health care dollars spent on traditional mental health services, and the growing promise of new funding for integrated health care and primary care services that offer better health outcomes at reasonable costs" (Goodheart, 2010, p. 194). Obviously astute competency for business management is no longer optional for mental health practitioners—it is a necessary ingredient for successful practice.

For whatever reason, it seems that mental health practitioners do not like to abide by well-established business and legal principles. The reason often voiced is that practitioners do not want to take the risk that goes with operating a business. Of course, few, if any, mental health training programs deal adequately with business management, which means that their graduates commonly do not know how to manage the business aspects of a mental health practice. As Goodheart says, "the time to make strategic transformative changes for the profession is now" (p. 194).

Mental health practitioners seem to have a special vulnerability to government actions (e.g., from a state department of revenue and the Internal Revenue Service) for improperly deeming associates as independent contractors, as opposed to employees. Under the sanctity of attorney-client confidentiality, countless mental health practitioners have acknowledged knowingly deeming an associate to be an "independent contractor" instead of the legally correct designation of "employee" because of a wish by both parties to avoid employment taxes! Mental health practitioners also are vulnerable to licensing boards and other agencies for wrongful division of revenues (i.e., a percentage arrangement that may constitute illegal fee-splitting). After being in practice for about a decade, a professional confessed to his or her attorney of having never heard of "illegal fee-splitting!

Rather than heeding the words of wisdom from an attorney or accountant, some practitioners rely on the faulty rationalization: "I know other mental health practitioners who do it this way," ignoring the axiom: "Two wrongs do not make a right." [For details about the issues of independent contractors versus employees and improper fee arrangements, see Woody (2011b).]

As an example of poor (dishonest?) judgment on the foregoing issue, a mental health practitioner rejected advice from several attorneys and accountants, and continued to deem numerous practitioners who worked under the practitioner's auspices "independent contractors." When government sources audited the practice, the mental health professional ended up paying both back taxes and a hefty penalty.

One senior mental health practitioner resisted legal advice about having an array of other mental health practitioners operating under a generic business name (e.g., "The XYZ Clinic"). The senior practitioner, wanting to avoid certain employment-related taxes, insisted that the other practitioners were independent contractors and were merely renting space and purchasing support service.

The practitioner was legally advised that reasonable consumers could potentially believe that the clinical situation was a team approach, which might create a duty for the senior "landlord" to maintain appropriate supervision—leaving the senior practitioner open to vicarious liability. Regardless, the "landlord" clung to the group name. When an associate committed malpractice and a large settlement was paid, the forecast of vicarious liability became a reality in the form of a lawsuit against the senior practitioner for inadequate supervision. The "landlord" also ended up paying a large settlement.

In my experience defending practitioners in this sort of situation, the foregoing scenarios are all too common. Professionalism does not accommodate ignorance or dishonesty. Not only should mental health practitioners receive legal, accounting, and other professional advice or counsel, they should rely on it.

Any enticement to create the notion in the minds of service users that there is a comprehensive mental health group (or even just a partnership) creates the specter of liability between the associated practitioners. Thus, any professional affiliation should be predicated on knowledge of the personal and professional qualities of everyone involved. To form an affiliation to "reduce overhead" is foolhardy.

Certainly the reputation of one practitioner has the potential to influence the reputation of affiliated practitioners. In a group of four mental health practitioners, there was a law suit against one of the practitioners for having had sexual relations with a client. Although the other three practitioners in the group certainly did not sanction the misconduct, the entire practice was cast into a negative light and revenues dropped precipitously—the group ended up disbanding.

To summarize, every mental health practitioner should know well any and all affiliates or colleagues. Regardless of training and experience, there should be supervision of every case. For vicarious liability, excuses only "dig the hole deeper," such as: "There was no way I could know what was going on behind my colleague's closed door." Legally, there are some situations that should not be allowed even if they seem expedient or alternatives cannot be easily afforded (e.g., lack of monitoring of colleagues to protect service users).

The legal challenge is usually to prove that due diligence was exercised to protect service users. If there is any indication of questionable qualities or practices, there should be written objections and corrective actions.

When employed by an organization, such as a community agency, clinic, school, or hospital, the mental health practitioner should require a detailed job description and have a contract that specifies the employer's legal liability (e.g., paying for personal legal services for the employee, as well as any settlement or judgment). A job description establishes whether an occurrence was within the scope of employment, thus making the employer potentially liable; and whether liability insurance is applicable. No matter how large or small the employing organization, a job description is an essential protective measure for both the employer and the employee.

A PROTECTIVE PRACTICE FRAMEWORK

A mental health practitioner should always be committed to the relevant professional ethics and operate by the standards and guidelines for delivery of the particular services in the given practice context. It is, of course, necessary to know all legal prescriptions and proscriptions, which underscores the need for ready counsel from an attorney and an accountant qualified in the particular jurisdiction. Given the liability of contemporary practice, to say "I cannot afford an attorney or an accountant" gives testimony to the fact that the professional may not be able to properly engage in practice.

Although modern mental health practices tend to be defined by national-level standards (as well as the laws and administrative code rules pertaining to the jurisdiction in which the services occur), there should be compatibility with public policy and community standards. Despite the temptation to "puff," as is commonly done by certain commercial sources, mental health professionals should be modest and factual in any promotional efforts. Although no longer unethical per se, adopting an aggrandizing fictitious name, such as the "International Center for Whatever Therapy," by one or only a few practitioners must be viewed as being of questionable professionalism. Also, if the name is misleading to a reasonable service user, it creates risks, as discussed previously in the chapter. It is advisable to use understatement for managing risk.

Modern mental health practice is a business not a benevolent service—even a non-profit organization operates as a business. There seems to be a tendency for some mental health practitioners to form a professional services corporation

> *Modern mental health practice is a business not a benevolent service—even a non-profit organization operates as a business.*

(often referred to as a P.A.) when there is little or no need for doing so. As one solo practitioner said, "I know that I do not need to be a corporation, I get no tax benefits, but I like to think it is a sign of legitimacy and that the public will be impressed." Seek legal advice as to whether there are adequate reasons to form a business entity.

Finally, as has been said throughout this book, within a mental health practice all operations should be in accord with a well-conceived risk-management system. Likewise, for business and career success, there must be wise and careful business planning to ensure quality care and legal operations.

CLIENT MANAGEMENT

An important theme throughout this book is that the mental health practitioner has a social responsibility and legal duty to establish and maintain an individualized treatment plan, to rely on evidence-based strategies, to keep comprehensive clinical and financial records, and to assiduously adhere to professional ethics and standards, as well as relevant laws and administrative code rules.

To best ensure quality care and risk management, the mental health practitioner should have a restrictive scope of service; trying to be all things to all people is unprofessional and risky. The practitioner should have a definite and documented competency for every aspect of the mental health services that are offered.

Quality care and risk management are gained by having written policies and definitions for standards and operational practices for each professional service [this notion is certainly inherent to the Health Insurance Portability and Accountability Act (HIPAA)]. To ensure protection for both the service user and practitioner, there should be a written service contract. The contract should use clear and practical language, and state the potential benefits and the limitations for a service—there should be no guaranteed outcome.

To some extent, the service contract should be tailored to the particular service user, relying on collaboration between the practitioner and the client. To avoid any misunderstanding later, all terms and conditions should be defined and explained fully to the service user; reminders may be merited. After offering legal information about a document to a practitioner, I often, with a supportive "teaching" tone, ask the practitioner to "now define and explain the document to me."

Because the individualized treatment plan evolves, objectives change, and strategies are eliminated or added, it is likely that there will be a need for a series of written informed consents rather than only a single document obtained at the outset of services.

Quality care and risk management also justify having oral and written consent for each and every aspect of professional service. Because the individualized treatment plan evolves, objectives change, and strategies are eliminated or added, it is likely that there will be a need for a series of written informed consents rather than only a single document obtained at the outset of services.

Acknowledging contemporary laws on mandatory reporting of possible child abuse, elder abuse, and vulnerable adult neglect and abuse, and the potential for subpoenas and court orders to require production of mental health information and records (which might have been protected in the past), each service user should receive and agree to both oral and written specification of the limits of confidentiality and privileged communication. Informed consent and authorizations for release of confidential information should be highly specific (what is to be released, to whom, and for what purpose) and contemporary (obtained after the information has been created).

In regard to a subpoena or court order, the mental health practitioner should provide the service user with written notice of the legal command, as this will allow the service user to potentially file a motion for a protective order. Also, with a valid subpoena or court order for the release of confidential information or documents, assuming that the service user has no objection to the practitioner's honoring the legal request, the mental health practitioner should obtain a written authorization for release of the documents or information from the service user. Although there are exceptions, the onus for objecting to a subpoena or court order generally is on the service user, not on the mental health practitioner.

The foregoing matters commonly require that the mental health practitioner consult with an attorney on a case-by-case basis. There may be legal issues about releasing mental health records and information that are unique to the particular jurisdiction in which the services occur. As mentioned several times before in this book, relying on legal advice from an attorney with a national professional organization or insurance company (who is not admitted to the bar in the jurisdiction in which the practice occurs) may be inadvisable—even if it is a free consultation provided by the organization or carrier.

Beyond the issues raised by a subpoena or court order, when releasing any mental health documents or information, it is prudent to have the service user review and approve all communications and documents that are going to others. I suggest that the mental health practitioner never write or release a psychological or clinical report that has not been reviewed by the service user. Implicit and explicit written informed consent and authorization to release confidential information will help preclude any sort of ethics or licensing complaint or legal challenge.

The preparation of mental health records must be compatible with the laws of the jurisdiction, as well as professional standards and ethics; unless subject to an exception, HIPAA also must be considered. There should be a standardized recording system, and the entries should reflect responses in as much detail as presumably would be relevant and material to the goals and objectives of the particular mental health services. As buttressed by professional ethics, standards, and laws, all records should be accurate and kept in secure storage with an efficient retrieval system.

> *There should be a standardized recording system, and the entries should reflect responses in as much detail as presumably would be relevant and material to the goals and objectives of the particular mental health services.*

Quality care and risk management require that all professional services be founded on a well-established theory (which is shared by a substantial portion of practitioners in the discipline) that is evidence based, and makes use of an assessment and diagnostic system. Prior to usage, any innovative technique should be reviewed and endorsed by other professionals. Service users should be informed verbally and by written policies of any reservations about effectiveness.

As discussed in Chapter Eight, there should be constant surveillance of every service user for any noncompliance, threats, or signs of danger or potential violence. Arrangements should be made in advance for reaching law enforcement and emergency services quickly if necessary.

For all service users, but especially those who are prone to be threatening, abusive, or violent behavior, there should be a written policy for termination. At the outset, this policy should be made available to potential service users and the policy should be patently clear that threats, abuse, or violence will not be tolerated. Also, all service users should be given a written policy on follow-up contacts.

Screening would-be service users in advance of services is an essential protective measure for quality care and risk management. It is appropriate for the practitioner to only accept clients for mental health services who have needs that are compatible with the practitioner's competency and the practice context, and who are willing and able to be compliant with a reasonable and evidence-based individualized treatment plan. Some would-be clients are not suitable for out-patient services from an independent practitioner, but instead may need in-patient or day-care services or may need to be under the auspices of a comprehensive mental health facility; thus, a referral system should be in place. The choice of a referral source should be determined by the needs of the service user, not by some business-related interest (e.g., not necessarily to a partner or associate).

Financial abuse of practitioners is commonplace. Along with screening for suitability for service, screening for financial ability to pay for the service is appropriate. It is well established that a practitioner's attempt to collect an overdue debt increases the likelihood of the "deadbeat" service user filing an ethics or licensing complaint, often with false information. This inclination sometimes extends to legal challenges (e.g., claiming damages due to alleged malpractice). Stated bluntly, although a practitioner can make use of collection agencies and law suits to collect overdue debts, it is better to simply not allow any service user to accrue a deficit in payments. Accounts should be monitored closely.

A "WARRIOR" MINDSET

The point has been made repeatedly that, for the sake of both quality care and risk management, mental health practitioners are neither required to nor should they give total deference to the preferences of service users. If a service user rejects an in-patient placement despite the practitioner's justified recommendation, the practitioner should view this as noncompliance by the service user and to continue providing service to the client may violate the practitioner's social responsibility and legal duty to maintain an appropriate individualized treatment plan.

Although collaboration in the treatment alliance is appropriate, the mental health professional must determine and control the services. Moreover, the practitioner cannot be expected to accept insults, risks, threats, danger, abuse, or violence, or sacrifice personal rights (e.g., never allow a client to intrude in the practitioner's zone of personal privacy or refuse to pay for services).

To achieve effective case management, the mental health practitioner must reflect confidence and competence. There should be no gesture that suggests an air of superiority, bravado, or one-upmanship. The "warrior" mindset relies on knowledge, skills, reason, and logic, and functioning as a reasonable, ordinary, and prudent practitioner.

> *The "warrior" mindset relies on knowledge, skills, reason, and logic, and functioning as a reasonable, ordinary, and prudent practitioner.*

Protection is gained from avoiding overexposure of personal qualities and opinions, cultivating positive relations with other health care providers in the community, and being a "professional" when communicating or dealing with past or present service users. When it comes to boundary issues, there is a solid argument for advocating that "once a service user, always a service user." Any semblance of a conflict of interests must be avoided. For example, the practitioner should avoid social or business relationships with members of a service user's immediate family.

When a complaint arises, the mental health practitioner should revert to a defensive posture. If an attorney is involved on behalf of a complainant, the practitioner should not respond with indignation or coyness. From day one of law school, attorneys are taught to deal with adversarial situations, whereas mental health practitioners are usually not trained for conflicts, disputes, or combat. The solution is simple: In the onslaught of an ethics or licensing complaint or a legal challenge, the practitioner should obtain and rely on wise legal counsel admitted to the bar in the jurisdiction in which the professional services occur.

Being steeped in academics and facing a challenge to self-esteem, some mental health practitioners foolishly impede legal efforts. Paraphrasing an old saying, the mental health practitioner who tries to self-manage his own legal case "has a fool for a client."

CONCLUSION

At the risk of sounding like a preacher, protection against ethics and licensing complaints and legal challenges is gained from not engaging in the seven deadly sins—pride, covetousness, lust, anger, gluttony, envy, and sloth—especially within any professional context or relationship. Moreover, two positive mantras for protection within the professional text are: (1) "Do no harm" and (2) "Do to others what you would have them do to you."

Finally, when sensing impending risks, threats, abuse, danger, or potential violence, the practitioner should stand firm for maintaining quality care, defending personal rights, and safeguarding professionalism. Said simply, goodness must prevail.

Epilogue

In the half-century plus that I have been involved with mental health services, the evolution of the related professional disciplines has been profound. For example, early on, it was believed that psychologists should not be in private practice or provide psychotherapy (unless supervised by a medical physician). In the intervening years, these notions have been soundly rejected by many professional and authoritative sources. Properly qualified mental health practitioners are now endorsed for an array of contextual and service options (e.g., in some jurisdictions, psychologists may earn prescription or "psychopharmacology" authority). The principle is simply: Change to benefit society is the *sine qua non* for professional services.

> *Properly qualified mental health practitioners are now endorsed for an array of contextual and service options (e.g., in some jurisdictions, psychologists may earn prescription or "psychopharmacology" authority). The principle is simply: Change to benefit society is the sine qua non for professional services.*

Being a professor and an independent practitioner, I am aware that the Ivory Tower and the Real World sometimes hold quite different views on the same subject. However, there can be no schism between higher education and mental health services. University and professional training programs must continue to promote learning that is based on behavioral science, and tailor the substance of the learning to prepare students and trainees to function effectively in the professional mission of furthering human welfare. As advocated in this book, there must be a unification of science and practice; the evidence-based approach, with support from empiricism when possible, is intended to accomplish quality care within a pragmatic framework.

Impressive research has advanced the mental health disciplines, academically and clinically. A concomitant has been the expansion of types of applications in an increasing variety of contexts, disciplines, and services. Mental health services have become a recognized part of public life, and any stigma attached to receiving mental health services has been reduced considerably.

Along the way, practitioners quested after licensure and third-party payments, presumably to meet a public need, but with an obvious wish for greater financial rewards. Predictably, consumer and financial stakeholders attracted the attention of the government and the legal system. The self-determining nature of the mental health professions suffered erosion. Today, the mental health disciplines are firmly embraced by the health care industry and subjected to intense scrutiny, with the potential for substantial penalties, by governmental (regulatory) and third-party payment sources. Accountability to multiple authorities is omnipresent.

Because there have been detailed explanations of the theories, public policies, laws, and research that underlie the principles, strategies, and guidelines relevant to quality care and risk management, redundancy is unnecessary at this point. However, there are several issues that merit reiteration. The following discussion should serve as a reminder of the myriad of topics presented in this book, and also provide a futuristic statement about mental health services.

The framework for the future of mental health services likely will be determined primarily by a national health care system. To date, its structure, governance, and functions are not determined. Service users and practitioners will have to adapt to government determinations, controls, and changes. There will be penalties for lack of cooperation or adherence to laws and policies. Through government endorsement, third-party payment sources may become the "driver of the bus."

The traditional definitions of professionalism and therapeutic alliance between service users and practitioners are antiquated. Professional services are within the realm of business and will be so even more in the future. This will require, of course, considerable adjustment by trainers and practitioners, and new attitudes, knowledge, and skills will be necessary. The people who seek training in mental health services cannot rely on humanistic devotion to helping; evidence-based competency and business acumen will be required.

The health care marketplace will fluctuate, and motivations for being a mental health practitioner will wax and wane, probably introducing new personal characteristics for the typical mental health professional (e.g., having more knowledge of neuroscience and business management). Although government regulation of the practitioners who violate the law is justified and essential for civility, the specter of more governmental regulation and legal impositions (including civil and criminal litigation) dampens the spirit of some practitioners.

Unless there is a major turnaround, members of a professional discipline will have less influence on practice issues; for example, the power attributed to professional associations has lessened and will diminish more in the future. Governmental priorities, with political agendas, will be determinative. Today's mental health practitioners (and their professional associations) should be girding for the forthcoming shifts in control.

Because mental health services are essential to the continued strength of society, there will, of course, be rewards (which cannot be predicted assuredly at this time). There is reason to believe that, to thrive, an affiliation of the practitioner with a health care collective (e.g., clinic, hospital, or defined practitioner group) will be expected. Although scholarship and research call for equality or parity between disciplines, social logic supports the idea that medicine will be viewed as being superior to all other health care disciplines. To many practitioners, this would be a "step backward," and merits professional attention immediately. Mental health services must become an essential sector of primary health care.

Given the concomitants of mental disorders and the social conditions (many of which have global influences), it seems probable (and desirable) that there will be a rebirth of many of the concepts that led to the community mental health ideas of the 1960s. That is, problems such as unemployment, homelessness, poverty, violence, drug abuse, and crime necessitate more outpatient, inpatient, and rehabilitation services, which will be venues for services from mental health practitioners.

Because quality care is a mandate, mental health services require reliance on scholarly and empirical evidence for planning programs and interventions—there can be no exceptions. Moreover, all services must be in accord with a carefully constructed (formal) individualized treatment plan, evaluated, modified, and fulfilled according to the needs of the particular service user, acceptable goals and objectives, and resources. Obviously, screening for admission, placement, continuance, and termination are cornerstones. All of the foregoing functions must be thoroughly documented, with protection of the clinical records to protect the service user's right of privacy.

Safeguards must be in place to guard against the inevitable psychological errors that every mental health practitioner makes. Greater use of outcome measures is necessary. Idiosyncratic values and biases are unacceptable. High-risk actions cannot be tolerated; impeccable assessment methods should be used to reduce risks. Interdisciplinary consensus about what constitutes quality care and risk management is required.

The foregoing issues prescribe that mental health practitioners, now and in the future, must be committed to excellence in personal and professional qualities. There can be no "resting on laurels"; there must be a pursuit of competency. Lifelong professional development supports the privilege of being a mental health practitioner. Beyond public policies and laws, professional ethics will be an essential dimension for practitioners and their decision making. Business ethics must be adapted to mental health services.

Contemporary conditions (and certainly those in the future, even more so) support creating a protective shield—precautionary measures—for society, service users, and practitioners. A defensive mindset is compatible with modern mental health services. The individualized treatment plan must include safeguards that address potential threats or violence, and the plan must specify legal options, such as mandatory reporting of certain types of abuse, reporting dangers to law enforcement, and conditions for termination of services due to noncompliance or unacceptable conduct. Protection of the rights of the mental health practitioner extends into his or her personal life, professional activities, home, and office. Neither verbal nor physical abuse can be tolerated. In every way, all interactions between service users and practitioners must be professional; there is reason to support the notion "once a service user, always a service user." I believe that any social, romantic, and commercial contacts between the service user (and the service user's immediate family) and the mental health practitioner are unacceptable in perpetuity.

The professional self-concept requires a strong sense of self-worth. Becoming a mental health practitioner should be viewed as a lifelong investment. The nature of professional services inevitably impacts on and drains from ego strength, although engaging in prosocial behavior also nurtures and increases ego strength. Having allies can bolster fortitude for dealing with taxing situations.

None of the foregoing is a condemnation of any source or aspect of mental health professionalism. Certainly there is no forecast of the lessening of importance or demise of the mental health disciplines. To the contrary, the modern-day complexities require greater reliance on scientifically oriented mental health services, but there will need to be evolutionary adaptations by all concerned. The proverbial bottom line is simple: When promoting mental health professionalism, the society, discipline, service user, and practitioner benefit from quality care and risk management.

References

Allport, G. W. (1942). *The use of personal documents in psychological science* (Bulletin 49). New York, NY: Social Science Research Council.

American Association for Marriage and Family Therapy. (2001). *AAMFT code of ethics.* Alexandria, VA: Author.

American Counseling Association. (2005). *ACA code of ethics.* Alexandria, VA: Author.

American Psychiatric Association. (1994). *Diagnostic and statistical manual of mental disorders* (4th ed., DSM-IV). Washington, DC: Author.

American Psychological Association. (2002). Ethical principles of psychologists and code of conduct. *American Psychologist, 57*(12), 1060–1073.

American Psychological Association Presidential Task Force on Evidence-Based Practice. (2006). Evidence-based practice in psychology. *American Psychologist, 61*(4), 271–285.

Aronson, E., Wilson, T. D., & Akert, R. M. (2007). *Social psychology* (6th ed.). Upper Saddle River, NJ: Pearson Prentice Hall.

Babiak, P., & Hare, R. D. (2006). *Snakes in suits: When psychopaths go to work.* New York, NY: HarperCollins.

Bandura, A. (1979). The social learning perspective: Mechanisms of aggression. In A. Toch (Ed.), *Psychology of crime and criminal justice* (pp. 298–336). New York, NY: Holt, Rinehart & Winston.

Barlow, D. H. (2010). Negative effects from psychological treatments. *American Psychologist, 65*(1), 13–20.

Barlow, D. H., & Nock, M. K. (2009). Why can't we be more ideographic in our research? *Perspectives on Psychological Science, 4,* 19–21.

Baron, J. E., & Shane, S. (2008). *Entrepreneurship: A process perspective.* New York, NY: Thomson-South-Western.

Baron, R. A., Byrne, D., & Branscombe, N. R. (2006). *Social psychology* (11th ed.). Boston, MA: Pearson Education.

Bartol, C. R., & Bartol, A. M. (2012). *Introduction to forensic psychology* (3rd ed.). Thousand Oaks, CA: Sage.

Benjamin, L. T., Jr. (2007). *A brief history of modern psychology*. Malden, MA: Blackwell.

Bennett, B. E., Bricklin, P. M., Harris, E., Knapp, S., VandeCreek, L., & Younggren, J. N. (2006). *Assessing and managing risk in psychological practice*. Rockville, MD: The Trust.

Bergin, A. E., & Strupp, H. H. (1972). *Changing frontiers in the science of psychotherapy*. Chicago, IL: Atherton.

Bloom, P. N. (1976). *Advertising, competition, and public policy*. Cambridge, MA: Ballinger.

Boyd, A. R., McLearen, A. M., Meyer, R. G., & Denney, R. L. (2007). *Detection of deception*. Sarasota, FL: Professional Resource Press.

Brint, S. (1994). *In an age of experts: The changing role of professionals in politics and public life*. Princeton, NJ: Princeton University Press.

Brock, G. W., & Barnard, C. P. (1999). *Procedures in marriage and family therapy* (3rd ed.). Boston, MA: Allyn and Bacon.

Bryman, A. (1992). *Charisma & leadership in organizations*. Newbury Park, CA: Sage.

Cardozo, B. N. (1921). *The nature of the judicial process*. New Haven, CT: Yale University Press.

Castonguay, L. G., Boswell, J. F., Constantino, M. J., Goldfried, M. R., & Hill, C. E. (2010). Training implications of harmful effects of psychological treatments. *American Psychologist, 65*(1), 34–49.

Cernozubov-Digman, K. (1997). Letter. *APA Monitor, 28*(6), 3 & 5.

Chance, P. L., & Chance, E. W. (2002). *Introduction to educational leadership & organizational behavior: Theory into practice*. Larchmont, NY: Eye on Education.

Charles, S. C., Wilbert, J. R., & Kennedy, E. C. (1984). Physician's self reports of reactions to malpractice litigation. *American Journal of Psychiatry, 141*(4), 563–565.

Chauvin, J.C., & Remley, T.P., Jr. (1996). Responding to allegations of unethical conduct. *Journal of Counseling and Development, 74*, 563–568.

Chwalisz, K. (2006). Statistical versus clinical prediction: From assessment to psychotherapy process and outcome. *Counseling Psychologist, 34*(3), 391–399.

Corey, M. S., & Corey, G. (2007). *Becoming a helper* (5th ed.). Belmont, CA: Thomson Brooks/Cole.

Corley, M. D. (2010). Staying out of trouble. *Family Therapy Magazine, 9*(4), 38–43.

Council for Exceptional Children. 1998. Retrieved from http://cec.sped.org/ps/code.html.

DeMatteo, D., Batastini, A., Foster, E., & Hunt, E. (2010). Individualizing risk assessment: Balancing idiographic and nomothetic data. *Journal of Forensic Psychology Practice, 10*(4), 360–371.

Dimidjian, S., & Hollon, S. D. (2010). How would we know if psychotherapy were harmful? *American Psychologist, 65*(1), 21–33.

Dingfelder, S. F. (2010). The first modern psychology study. *Monitor on Psychology, 41*(7), 30–31.

Dishion, T. J., & Stormshak, E. A. (2007). *Intervening in children's lives: An ecological, family-centered approach to mental health care.* Washington, DC: American Psychological Association.

Domino, G. (2000). *Psychological testing: An introduction.* Upper Saddle River, NJ: Prentice-Hall.

Drogin, E. Y., Connell, M., Foote, W. E., & Sturm, C. A. (2010). The American Psychological Association's revised "Record Keeping Guidelines": Implications for the practitioner. *Professional Psychology, 41*(3), 236–243.

Drucker, P. F. (1974). *Management: Tasks, responsibilities, and practices.* New York, NY: Harper and Row.

Dutton, D. G. (2003). *The abusive personality: Violence and control in intimate relationships.* New York, NY: Guilford.

Edwards, A. J. (1964). Social desirability and performance on the MMPI. *Psychometrika, 29*, 295–308.

Elliott, F. (1977). The neurology of explosive rage: The episodic dyscontrol syndrome. In M. Roy (Ed.), *Battered women: A psychosociological study of domestic violence* (pp. 98–109). New York, NY: Van Nostrand.

Federal Trade Commission. (1979). *Federal Trade Commission Decisions, 94,* 701–1041 [based largely on *American Medical Association v. FTC,* 94 FTC 701, final order, October 12, 1979].

Feinman, J. M. (2010*). Law 101: Everything you need to know about American law* (3rd ed.). New York, NY: Oxford University Press.

Fisher, C. B. (2009). *Decoding the ethics code* (2nd ed.). Thousand Oaks, CA: Sage.

Fiske, S. T. (2004). *Social beings: A core motives approach to social psychology.* Hoboken, NJ: John Wiley.

Franzoi, S. L. (2009). *Social psychology* (5th ed.). Boston, MA: McGraw-Hill.

Fullan, M., Miles, M. B., & Taylor, G. (1980). Organizational development in schools: The state of the art. *Review of Educational Research, 50*(1), 121–183.

Goodheart, C. D. (2010). Economics and psychology practice: What we need to know and why. *Professional Psychology, 41*(3), 189–195.

Gove, P. B. (Ed.). (1961). *Webster's new third international dictionary of the English language unabridged.* Springfield, MA: G. & C. Merriam.

Groopman, J. (2007). *How doctors think.* Boston, MA: Houghton Mifflin.

Guy, J. D., Brown, C. K., & Poelstra, P. L. (1990). Who gets attacked? A national survey of patient violence directed at psychologists in clinical practice. *Professional Psychology, 21*(6), 493–495.

Havelock, R. G. (1973). *The change agent's guide to innovation in education.* Englewood Cliffs, NJ: Educational Technology Publications.

Hogan, R., & Smither, R. (2008). *Personality: Theories and applications* (2nd ed.). Tulsa, OK: Hogan Press.

Hoy, W. K., & Miskel, C. G. (1996). *Educational administration: Theory, research, and practice* (5th ed.). New York, NY: McGraw-Hill.

Huesmann, L. R., Moise-Titus, J., Podolski, C. L., & Eron, L. D. (2003). Longitudinal relations between children's exposure to TV violence and their aggressive and violent behavior in young adulthood: 1977–1992. *Developmental Psychology, 39*(2), 201–221.

Johnson, W. B., & Ridley, C. R. (2008). *The elements of ethics for professionals*. New York, NY: Palgrave Macmillan.

Kassin, S., Fein, S., & Markus, H. R. (2011). *Social psychology* (8th ed.). Belmont, CA: Wadsworth, Cengage Learning.

Keeton, W. P., Dobbs, D. B., Keeton, R. E., & Owen, D. G. (1984) *Prosser and Keeton on the Law of Torts* (5th ed.). St. Paul, MN: West.

Kirkland, K., & Kirkland, K. L. (2001). Frequency of child custody evaluation complaints and related disciplinary action: A survey of the association of state and provincial psychology boards. *Professional Psychology, 32*(2), 171–174.

Knapp, S. J., & VandeCreek, L. (1997). *Treating patients with memories of abuse: Legal risk management*. Washington, DC: American Psychological Association.

Koocher, G. P., & Keith-Spiegel, P. (2008). *Ethics in psychology and the mental health professions: Standards and cases* (3rd ed.). New York, NY: Oxford University Press.

Lanyon, R. I., & Goodstein, L. D. (1997). *Personality assessment* (3rd ed.). New York, NY: Wiley.

Lyman, H. B. (1978). *Test scores and what they mean* (3rd ed.). Englewood Cliffs, NJ: Prentice-Hall.

Lyman, H. B. (1991). *Test scores and what they mean* (5th ed.). Boston, MA: Allyn and Bacon.

Maslow, A. H. (1970). *Motivation and personality*. New York, NY: Harper & Row.

Matarazzo, J. D. (1990). Psychological assessment versus psychological testing: Validation from Binet to school, clinic and courtroom. *American Psychologist, 45*, 999–1017.

McCall, R. J. (1976). The defense mechanisms re-examined. In W. Katkovsky & L. Gorlow (Eds.), *The psychology of adjustment* (3rd ed., pp. 270–284). New York, NY: McGraw-Hill.

McDaniel, S. W., Smith, L. J., & Smith, K. T. (1986). The status of physician advertising. *Journal of Professional Services Marketing, 2*(1/2), 131–145.

McHugh, R. K., & Barlow, D. H. (2010). The dissemination and implementation of evidence-based psychological treatments. *American Psychologist, 62*(2), 73–84.

Meehl, P. E. (1954). *Clinical versus statistical prediction: A theoretical analysis and a review of the evidence*. Minneapolis, MN: University of Minneapolis Press.

Meehl, P. E. (1956). Wanted—A good cookbook. *American Psychologist, 11*, 263–272.

Meloy, J. R. (1992). *Violent attachments*. Northvale, NJ: Aronson.

Murdick, N.L., Gartin, B.C., & Crabtree, T. (2007). *Special education law* (2nd ed.). Upper Saddle River, NJ: Pearson (Merrill Prentice Hall).

Myers, D. G. (2005). *Social psychology* (8th ed.). Boston, MA: McGraw-Hill.

National Association of Social Workers. (1999). *Code of ethics* (Rev. ed.). Washington, DC: Author.

Norcross, J. C., Freedheim, D. K., & VandenBos, G. R. (2011). Into the future: Retrospect and prospect in psychotherapy. In J. C. Norcross, G. R. VandenBos, & D. K. Freedheim (Eds.), *History of psychotherapy: Continuity and change* (2nd ed., pp. 743–760). Washington, DC: American Psychological Association.

Norhouse, P. G. (2009). *Introduction to leadership concepts and practice*. Thousand Oaks, CA: Sage.

Organista, P. B., Marin, G., & Chun, K. M. (2010). *The psychology of ethnic groups in the United States.* Los Angeles, CA: Sage.

Peterson, M. B. (2001). Recognizing concerns about how some licensing boards are treating psychologists. *Professional Psychology: Research and Practice, 32*(4), 339–340.

Pipes, R. B., Holstein, J. E., & Aguirre, M. G. (2005). Examining the personal-professional distinction: Ethics codes and the difficulty of drawing a boundary. *American Psychologist, 60*(4), 325–334.

Pope, K. S., & Vasquez, M. J. T. (2011). *Ethics in psychotherapy and counseling: A practical guide* (4th ed.). San Francisco, CA: Jossey-Bass (John Wiley).

Price, M. (2010). Sins against science. *Monitor of Psychology, 41*(7), 44–47.

Reaves, R. P., & Ogloff, J. R. P. (1996). Liability for professional misconduct. In L. J. Bass, S. T. DeMers, J. R. P. Ogloff, C. Peterson, J. L. Pettifor, R. P. Reaves, T. Rétfalvi, N. P. Simon, C. Sinclair, & R. M. Tipton (Eds.), *Professional conduct and discipline in psychology* (pp. 117–142). Washington, DC: American Psychological Association; and Montgomery, AL: Association of State and Provincial Psychology Boards.

Robertson, M. H., & Woody, R. H. (1997). *Theories and method for practice of clinical psychology.* Madison, CT: International Universities Press.

Rogers, C. R. (1961). *On becoming a person.* Boston, MA: Houghton Mifflin.

Schachter, S. (1964). The interaction of cognitive and physiological determinants of emotional state. In L. Berkowitz (Ed.), *Advances in experimental social psychology* (Vol. 1, pp. 49–80). New York, NY: Academic Press.

Shapiro, D. L., & Smith, S. R. (2011). *Malpractice in psychology.* Washington, DC: American Psychological Association.

Shedler, J. (2010). The efficacy of psychodynamic psychotherapy. *American Psychologist, 65*(2), 98–109.

Silver, E. (2006). Understanding the relationship between mental disorder and violence: The need for a criminological perspective. *Law and Human Behavior, 30*(6), 685–706.

Simpson, J. A., & Weiner, E. S. C. (1989). *The Oxford English dictionary, Vol. 12* (2nd ed.). New York, NY: Oxford University Press.

Slovenko, R. (1973). *Psychiatry and law.* Boston, MA: Little, Brown.

Sokal, M. M. (1992). Origins and early years of the American Psychological Association, 1890–1906. *American Psychologist, 47,* 111–122.

Spohn, C., & Hemmens, C. (2009). *Courts.* Thousand Oaks, CA: Sage

Sternberg, R. J. (2009). A new model for teaching ethical behavior. (Chronicle Review, April 24) *Chronicle of Higher Education, 55*(33), B14–15.

Stewart, A. E. (2010). Explorations in the meanings of excellence and its importance to counselors: The culture of excellence in the United States. *Journal of Counseling & Development, 88,* 189–195.

Tarasoff v. Regents of the University of California, 17 Cal. 3d 425, 551 P.2d 334, 131 Cal. Rptr. 14 (Cal. 1976).

Teplin, L. A. (1986, April). *Keeping the peace: The parameters of police discretion in relation to the mentally disordered.* Washington, DC: U.S. Department of Justice, National Institute of Justice.

Teplin, L. A. (2000, July). Police discretion and mentally ill persons. *National Institute of Justice Journal*, No. 244, 8–15.

Thorne, F. C. (1961). *Clinical judgment: A study of clinical error*. Brandon, VT: *Journal of Clinical Psychology*.

VandenBos, G. R. (Ed.). (2007). *APA dictionary of psychology*. Washington, DC: American Psychological Association.

Van Ornum, W., Dunlap, L. L., & Shore, M. F. (2008). *Psychological testing across the life span*. Upper Saddle River, NJ: Pearson (Prentice-Hall).

Walfish, S., & Barnett, J. E. (2009). *Financial success in mental health practice*. Washington, DC: American Psychological Association.

Walker, M. (1979). *Advertising and promoting the professional practice*. New York, NY: Hawthorn.

Walsh, W. B., & Betz, N. E. (2001). *Tests and assessment* (4th ed.). Upper Saddle River, NJ: Prentice-Hall.

Watson, J. C., Goldman, R. N., & Greenberg, L. S. (2011). Humanistic and experiential theories of psychotherapy. In J. C. Norcross, G. R. VandenBos, & D. K. Freedheim (Eds.), *History of psychotherapy: Continuity and change* (2nd ed., pp. 141–172). Washington, DC: American Psychological Association.

Welch, B. L. (2010). Triple jeopardy: Dangers of an APA ethics complaint. *National Psychologist, 19*(4), 15.

Westen, D., & Weinberger, J. (2004). When clinical description becomes statistical prediction. *American Psychologist, 59*(7), 595–613.

Wierzbicki, M. (1993). *Issues in clinical psychology: Subjective versus objective approaches*. Boston, MA: Allyn and Bacon.

Williams, M. H. (2001). The question of psychologists' maltreatment by state licensing boards: Overcoming denial and seeking remedies. *Professional Psychology: Research and Practice, 32*(4), 341–344.

Woody, R. H. (1988a). *Fifty ways to avoid malpractice: A guidebook for the mental health practitioner*. Sarasota, FL: Professional Resource Exchange.

Woody, R. H. (1988b). *Protecting your mental health practice: How to minimize legal and financial risk*. San Francisco, CA: Jossey-Bass.

Woody, R. H. (1989). *Business success in mental health practice: Modern marketing, management and legal strategies*. San Francisco, CA: Jossey-Bass.

Woody, R. H. (1991). *Quality care in mental health services: Assuring the best clinical services*. San Francisco, CA: Jossey-Bass.

Woody, R. H. (1993). Regulatory equality for clients and psychotherapists. *Voices: The Art and Science of Psychotherapy, 29*(2), 87–92.

Woody, R. H. (1996). Dangerous patients: The therapist as "weaponless policeman." *Journal of Psychohistory, 23*(4), 438–446.

Woody, R. H. (1998). Dubious and bogus credentials in mental health practice. *Ethics & Behavior, 7*(4), 337–345.

Woody, R. H. (2000a). *Child custody: Practice standards, ethical issues, legal safeguards for mental health professionals*. Sarasota, FL: Professional Resource Press.

Woody, R. H. (2000b). What to do upon receiving a complaint. In L. VandeCreek & T. L. Jackson (Eds.), *Innovations in clinical practice: A source book* (Vol. 18, pp. 213–229). Sarasota, FL: Professional Resource Press.

Woody, R. H. (2005). Defending against legal complaints. In G. P. Koocher, J. C. Norcross, & S. S. Hill, III (Eds.), *Psychologists' desk reference* (2nd ed., pp. 565–566). New York, NY: Oxford University Press.

Woody, R. H. (2007). Bogus and dubious credentials revisited: Professionalism requires action. *Independent Practitioner, 27*(3), 140–141.

Woody, R. H. (2008). Obtaining legal counsel for child and family mental health services. *American Journal of Family Therapy, 36*(4). 323–331.

Woody, R. H. (2009a). Economic sustainability: You get what you pay for. *Independent Practitioner, 29*(4), 209–210.

Woody, R. H. (2009b). Psychological injury from licensing complaints against mental health practitioners. *Personal Injury and Law, 2*, 1009–113.

Woody, R. H. (2011a). The financial conundrum for mental health practice. *American Journal of Family Therapy, 39*(1), 1–10.

Woody, R. H. (2011b). Letters of protection: Ethical and legal financial considerations. *Journal of Forensic Psychology Practice, 11*(4). 361–367.

World Health Organization World Mental Health Survey Consortium. (2004). Prevalence, severity, and unmet need for treatment of mental disorders in the World Health Organization world mental health surveys. *Journal of the American Medical Association, 291*, 2581–2590.

Zuckerman, E. L. (2006). *HIPAA help: A compliance toolkit for psychotherapists for maintaining records' privacy and security, managing risks, and operating ethically and; legally under HIPAA* (Rev. ed.). Ambrust, PA: Three Wishes Press.

Index